American
Heart
Association®

Instant & Healthy

Also by the American Heart Association

The New American Heart Association Cookbook, 9th Edition
American Heart Association Healthy Fats, Low-Cholesterol Cookbook, 5th Edition
American Heart Association Grill It, Braise It, Broil It
American Heart Association Go Fresh
American Heart Association Healthy Slow Cooker Cookbook
American Heart Association Eat Less Salt
American Heart Association Quick & Easy Cookbook, 2nd Edition
American Heart Association Low-Salt Cookbook, 4th Edition
American Heart Association Healthy Family Meals

Minestrone Soup,
page 48

American
Heart
Association.

Instant & Healthy

100 Low-Fuss,
High-Flavor Recipes for Your
Pressure Cooker,
Multicooker
& Instant Pot®

Harmony Books
New York

Published in the United States by Harmony Books,
an imprint of the
Crown Publishing Group, a division of
Penguin Random House LLC,
New York.
crownpublishing.com

Harmony Books is a registered trademark and the Circle
colophon is a trademark of Penguin Random House LLC.

Your contributions to the American Heart Association
support research that helps make publications like this
possible. For more information, call 1-800-AHA-USA1
(1-800-242-8721) or contact us online at heart.org.

Library of Congress Cataloging-in-Publication Data
has been applied for.

ISBN 978-0-525-57554-2
Ebook ISBN 978-0-525-57555-9

Printed in the United States of America

Design by Jan Derevjanik
Photographs by Lauren Volo

First Edition

Acknowledgments

American Heart Association Consumer Publications
Managing Editor: Deborah Renza Puccio
Content Manager: Roberta Westcott Sullivan

Recipe Developers
Kathryn Moore
Roxanne Wyss

Nutrition Analyst
Tammi Hancock, R.D.

Chicken Shawarma,
page 85

Contents

Fish Tacos with Broccoli Slaw,
page 69

Introduction

Welcome to the world of healthy cooking using your electric pressure cooker or multicooker! With your pressure cooker or multicooker and this cookbook, you'll be making nutritious, delicious foods that are easy to prepare and cook more quickly than with many traditional cooking methods.

Home cooks have been using stovetop pressure cookers for decades to prepare foods, but these original cookers required making adjustments to the heat to regulate the pressure as needed. Today's electric pressure cookers are preset and automatic, so you don't have to guess at the heat setting and you can set the timer so you can do other tasks without fussing over the cooker.

Multicookers are usually pressure cookers, but not all electric pressure cookers are multicookers. A multicooker is just what the name implies—a versatile, jack-of-all trades kitchen appliance. The features and settings vary by the brand, but typically they are pressure cookers with additional settings for slow cooking, steaming, sautéing, and even cooking rice and making yogurt, among other techniques. A benefit of this appliance is that you have only one device to learn how to use and to store in your kitchen. This appliance is the new modern-kitchen workhorse that you'll want to use often.

Using a multicooker on the pressure cooker setting and using an electric pressure cooker are quite similar, so the cooking times and the tasty food that results will be the same. However, using a stovetop pressure cooker will require different cooking times and may give different results. All of the recipes in this book were tested in electric pressure cookers or multicookers, not in stovetop pressure cookers. When the recipes call for using a "pressure cooker," this refers to the pressure setting on your electric pressure cooker or multicooker. All of the recipes in this cookbook were developed for and tested in a 6-quart multicooker or electric pressure cooker. If you have a larger or smaller appliance, you'll need to adjust the recipes for best results.

The Instant Pot® is one popular brand of multicooker and because it's so common, you may hear people refer to this appliance category by that brand name. (It's similar to when people refer to a tissue as a Kleenex® or call a slow cooker a Crock Pot®; these are all brand names and are registered trademarks.) However, there are other brands of multicookers on the market, including ones from Cuisinart, Fagor, Breville, and Tristar, among others, offering different models and features. Choose the appliance that best suits your budget and needs. The recipes in this cookbook will be successful with any brand.

BENEFITS OF PRESSURE COOKING

Quick cooking Each recipe in this book includes the time it will take for you to prepare the dish, from chopping the ingredients to letting pressure build, cooking, and releasing pressure. Pressure cookers work by building up steam, which cooks foods more quickly. The boiling point of water is 212°F, but in a pressure cooker the temperature of the liquid rises to approximately 250°F. The result? Faster cooking, which means less time in the kitchen for you and food on the table more quickly for your family. So, for example, in a pressure cooker dried beans take 30 to 45 minutes to cook whereas when prepared on the stovetop they can take hours—and that's in addition to soaking them ahead of time. The same is true for many other foods, too, such as beef brisket. Using a pressure cooker, you'll have a tender, moist piece of meat in less than an hour. If you cook the brisket in the oven, it'll take hours.

Great flavor Pressure-cooked foods often are more flavorful than foods cooked with other cooking techniques because in a pressure cooker the flavors are concentrated under pressure. The results? Less need to add unwanted sodium and "bad" fats to flavor the food.

Safe and efficient Today's electric pressure cookers and multicookers have interlocking lids and are engineered for safe, efficient cooking. Gone are the days when the buildup of too much pressure inside the pot forced the lid off, resulting in a dangerous situation and food everywhere.

Variety You can cook a variety of foods easily and deliciously in a pressure cooker. Since pressure cooking uses moist heat to cook, it's an ideal way to cook soups, stews, dried beans, sauces, and any dish that you'd typically braise or simmer.

Ten Steps to Successful Pressure Cooking

1. **Get familiar with your appliance.** Be sure to read the instructional manual that comes with your pressure cooker or multicooker. Each model has various settings and features and uses unique terms to describe them. Familiarize yourself with the design, location of the settings, and the terms used for your particular cooker so you can quickly and easily select the setting you need, lock the lid, and seal and release the pressure.

2. **Use your appliance safely.** Follow the manufacturer's directions for your electric pressure cooker or multicooker explicitly and carefully, especially regarding safety procedures, recommended settings, foods to avoid cooking, maximum fill lines, and minimum amounts of water to use in each recipe. Some multicookers state to avoid cooking dried beans, split peas, rhubarb, oatmeal, pasta, applesauce, cranberries, and other foods that may clog valves or cause splatters. Follow the recommendations for your brand and model carefully. Your safety and the proper operation of your particular appliance take precedence over the information and recipes provided in this cookbook. If your model cautions against cooking a certain food in the appliance, do not attempt to cook it. If in doubt or if you have questions, contact the manufacturer of your cooker.

3. **Select a recipe and read it through completely.** By familiarizing yourself with the recipe, you won't have any surprises once you get cooking. Prep the ingredients before you turn on the cooker so once it's on you're all ready to go.

4. **Sauté or brown the food as needed.** As a first step in many pressure cooking recipes, it's common to add a small amount of oil to sauté (using the sauté, brown, or bottom heat setting) aromatic vegetables, such as onions and garlic, or brown chicken or meat. This is an extra step, but it adds a great deal of flavor to the overall dish. When sautéing, do not cover the pressure cooker and do stir the food frequently. Sautéing in a pressure cooker is similar to browning in a skillet on the stovetop, so be sure to use caution since the pan and food will be hot and the food can splatter. Turn off the pressure cooker after sautéing.

5. **Put the ingredients in the pressure cooker.** Generally, do not fill a pressure cooker more than about two-thirds full and never exceed the max fill line.

6. **Add the liquid.** A pressure cooker must have some liquid, often at least 1 cup or more, to operate properly. The liquid may be water or broth or come from watery foods, such as tomatoes.

7. **Check the gasket and secure the lid.** It's important that the silicone gasket be in place correctly and the interlocking lid is secured. (Usually this means that once the lid and base are engaged you can rotate the lid to lock it in place.) The lid must be properly locked and the steam vent closed to build the pressure.

8. **Select the setting and set the timer.** Often, this means to first set the appliance on manual and high pressure. Next, set the timer. The timer does not begin its countdown until the appliance reaches pressure. So, for example, if a recipe states to set the cooker on high pressure for 10 minutes, it may take 5 to 10 minutes to build up the pressure. During this time, the readout may simply state "on." It's normal to see and hear some steam escape. Once the cooker reaches the correct pressure, steam will not escape, and the timer will start counting down. When the time has elapsed, many multicookers automatically turn on the warm setting. You may want to turn off the pressure cooker or even unplug it.

9. **Release the pressure.** The safety mechanism prevents the lid from opening until the pressure has been released. Use caution and keep your hands and face away as you release the pressure. There are three ways to release pressure; the one you use depends on the recipe or food you're cooking.

   • **QUICK RELEASE** Quickly releasing the pressure is called for when additional cooking may cause overcooking. Typically, this means that you rotate the pressure release to "vent." You'll hear the steam escape; be sure to keep your hands and face away from the hot steam.

   • **NATURAL RELEASE** As the pressure cooker cools off, the pressure will decrease naturally on its own. This is the common choice to use when cooking broths, grains, beans, meats, and foods that benefit from the slower cooling time or extended cooking time or foods that may cause the steam to splatter. Allow plenty of time for this step as it may take from 15 to 30 minutes, or even longer, for the pressure to be released.

   • **NATURAL RELEASE AND QUICK RELEASE** Sometimes recipes call for releasing the pressure naturally for 5 to 15 minutes, then to vent it to quickly release any remaining pressure. This is a convenient way to allow for a slightly extended cooking time yet save a bit of time as well as prevent splatters.

10. **Remove the lid.** Use caution and carefully lift the lid by tilting it away from you so any residual steam or the water that typically condenses on the lid can safely escape. Transfer the food to plates and enjoy a healthy, delicious home-cooked meal.

Cooking Tips for Best Results

- Measure all of the ingredients carefully, especially the water or broth. The cooking time in the recipe is based on the volume of food, so any change can affect the cooking time.

- As cooking goes quickly, be sure to gather all the ingredients and complete all the prep work, such as chopping or slicing ingredients, rounding up the spices from the pantry, and measuring the liquid, before turning on the pressure cooker.

- For uniform cooking, cut the food into similar-size pieces.

- Check the manufacturer's information for cooking charts for common foods. These make it easy for you to use your pressure cooker for a wide array of vegetables, meats, rice, and more.

- When the recommended cooking time is up, if you find that the food is not as cooked as you'd like it to be, you can re-cover the pressure cooker and cook the food longer. To do so, secure the lid, set to pressure cook, and set the timer for only a few minutes—3 to 5 minutes. To prevent overcooking, do not use long extended times. When the extra time is complete, release the pressure as originally directed. Once you have used your pressure cooker a few times and tried a few recipes, you'll know if the cooking times need to be adjusted for your particular model of pressure cooker or your personal preferences.

- When calculating how long it takes for food to be ready to serve, remember to include the time it takes to heat up the cooker, cook the food, and release the pressure. For example, if a recipe states to cook on high pressure for 10 minutes, it may take 5 to 10 minutes to build up the pressure before the timer begins counting. After cooking, if the recipe calls for releasing the pressure naturally for 10 minutes, then quick-releasing the remaining pressure, the total time from start to finish will be about 30 minutes. If you use the sauté setting at the beginning of the recipe, add another 5 minutes to the total cooking time. Every recipe in this book calculates the total time, which includes prep, cooking, and time to build and release pressure.

- Many cookers have preset functions or settings, such as soup, meat, or beans. This allows the cooker to automatically choose the temperature and pressure that the manufacturer recommends to best cook that particular food. If your unit has these settings, try them for a similar type of dish and evaluate the results. For example, if the soup recipe you're making calls for high pressure, you can choose to use the soup setting instead if it's available on your appliance. Or, conversely, if a recipe calls for using the soup setting and your appliance doesn't have that setting, then you can use the manual/high pressure setting. These settings often have preset cooking times, so if you do use those settings for any of the recipes in this cookbook, use the cooking time called for in the recipe.

- Do not use an electric pressure cooker or multicooker for canning foods.

Tips for Easy Cleanup

- Follow the manufacturer's manual for cleaning your cooker. Some parts may be dishwasher safe, but check the manual. A small brush may help to clean around the edge of the lid. Do not immerse the heating base in water.

- The silicone gasket in the lid must be kept clean. If you cook strong-smelling or aromatic foods, it can retain the odors. To minimize that, remove the gasket and wash and dry it thoroughly. Soaking the gasket in a mixture of distilled white vinegar and water and washing it well will help prevent odors. To prevent any odor transfer to other foods, purchase an extra gasket so you can use one when cooking fish or curry and keep one for making yogurt or other more mild-flavored foods.

- If your cooking pot is stainless steel and food residues stick to the pot, try a nonabrasive appliance cleaner/polish or cleaning powder to clean the surface without scratching it.

ACCESSORIES

Steaming rack or basket Many pressure cookers come with a steaming rack. If yours didn't, you'll need to purchase a small, round metal rack or inexpensive steaming basket to use when cooking some of the recipes. Racks or baskets are a convenient way to hold fish or keep vegetables out of liquid and are required if you're using a bowl or pan in your pressure cooker.

Bowl Some recipes recommend using a ceramic or glass heat-proof bowl. A 6- to 7-cup bowl is often the ideal size. Be sure the bowl is heat-proof and check that it fits inside the pressure cooker before you begin preparing the recipe. Fill the bowl no more than two-thirds full and place it on the rack in the pressure cooker. Use an aluminum foil sling (see page 15) to make it easy to lower the bowl into the pressure cooker and also take it out.

Pan A small, heat-proof pan is needed for some recipes. A 7-inch springform pan is convenient. Check that it fits inside the pressure cooker before you begin preparing the recipe. Fill the pan no more than two-thirds full and place it on the rack in the pressure cooker. Use an aluminum foil sling (see page 15) to make it easy to lower the pan into the pressure cooker and also take it out. If preparing a moist food in the pan, line the pan with cooking parchment to prevent leaking.

Aluminum foil sling To make it safe and easy to lower a bowl or pan into the pressure cooker and then take it out, cut an 18-inch-long piece of aluminum foil. Fold it lengthwise in thirds to make a ribbon about 4 x 18 inches. Place the filled bowl or pan in the center of the ribbon and draw the ends of the foil ribbon up and over the bowl or pan. Use the foil as a sling to lower the bowl or pan into the pressure cooker. Leave the foil sling in place under the bowl or pan so you can use it to safely lift it out when cooking has finished.

Healthy Cooking

- Pressure cookers are an ideal appliance to cook whole grains, beans, fruits, vegetables, soups, stews, poultry, extra-lean and lean meats, skinless poultry, and seafood.

- Be sure to trim and discard all visible fat before placing the food in the pressure cooker.

- Sautéing food adds color and flavor so it's worth doing this step even if it takes a bit more time to complete your dish. Be sure to use a healthy (nontropical) vegetable oil, such as canola, corn, or olive oil, and measure it so you use no more than 2 to 3 teaspoons. If your cooker is stainless steel (NOT nonstick coated), you can lightly coat the cooking pot with cooking spray instead of using oil, if you prefer.

- Use plenty of fresh or dried herbs and other sodium-free flavorings, such as lemon juice or vinegar, in place of added salt. When pressure cooking, both fresh and dried herbs can be added at the beginning of cooking. Sprinkle with additional fresh herbs before serving, if desired.

- Many of the recipes in this cookbook call for broth. Make your own fat-free, low-sodium broths and stocks by making and freezing Chicken Stock (page 39), Beef Stock (page 40), and Vegetable Broth (page 41) so you'll have them on hand when you need them.

Herbed Chicken and
Root Vegetables, page 78

Healthy For Good™

Healthy For Good™ is a revolutionary movement built to help you make lasting changes to your health and life, one small step at a time. The approach is simple: *Eat Smart. Add Color. Move More. Be Well.*

EAT SMART.

Eating healthy doesn't have to mean dieting or giving up all the foods you love. You'll learn how to ditch the junk food and give your body the nutrient-dense fuel it needs.

Healthy Eating Starts at Home

Cooking more meals at home gives everyone in the family an opportunity to build better eating habits, one plate at a time.

- Sit down and eat as a family to help ensure healthy and balanced meals.

- Build your cooking skills so you can control what ingredients are used and the amount of sodium in your food.

- Keep your kitchen stocked with fruits, vegetables, lean protein, and whole grains to add true nourishment to your life.

Take Control of Your Portions

A portion is how much we choose to eat. Portions are 100 percent under our control and learning how to eat smart portions is a big part of eating healthier.

- Read nutrition labels carefully to compare serving size, calories, sodium levels, and added sugars.

- Eat reasonable portions, even when you're served more than you need.

- Prepare and eat more meals at home so you can control the ingredients and portion size.

Build a Better Plate

Eating healthy starts with putting the right foods on your plate, in the right amounts. An easy way to have more energy is to make smart food choices.

- Include fruits and veggies, whole grains, beans and legumes, nuts and seeds, lean protein, fat-free/low-fat dairy products, and healthy fats.

- Limit sweets, fatty or processed meats, solid fats such as butter, and salty or highly processed foods.

- Avoid partially hydrogenated oils.

Fats Aren't All Bad

Your body needs fats but some are better than others. Replace bad fats with healthier ones to keep your body nourished.

- Healthier unsaturated fats come from nontropical liquid oils, nuts and seeds, avocados, and fatty fish.

- Bad fats are solid or saturated fats; they come from animal sources such as meat and dairy as well as tropical oils such as coconut and palm.

- Avoid trans fats and partially hydrogenated oils, found in some processed foods.

A Healthy Diet Without Dieting

Go for a simple, no-fad healthy eating pattern to nourish your body and bring out the best you.

- Concentrate on smaller portions, rather than forcing yourself to eliminate foods you love.

- Add fiber-rich foods that will keep you feeling full, such as whole grains, legumes, vegetables, and fruits.

- Don't buy empty-calorie foods and sugary drinks; if they aren't in your pantry, then you're less likely to indulge.

Make Healthier Choices with the Heart-Check Mark

Foods certified by the American Heart Association are recommended for an overall healthy diet pattern.

- Foods bearing our Heart-Check mark have been certified to meet our nutrition requirements.

- Look for the mark on packaging in grocery stores.

- Check to see if your favorite brand is certified at heartcheck.org.

Peach Crisp,
page 185

ADD COLOR.

An easy first step to eating healthy is to include fruits and vegetable at every meal or snack. All forms (fresh, frozen, canned, and dried) and colors count, so go ahead and add color to your plate—and your life.

Easy on the Budget

You don't have to break the bank to get fruits and veggies on your plate; just add a little at a time and look for ways to save.

- Many fruits and vegetables cost less than $1 per serving.

- Single-serving fruit and vegetables can be cheaper than vending machine snacks.

- Buying produce in bulk and freezing the excess can help you save in the long run.

Knock Out the Added Salt and Sugar

Canned, frozen, and dried fruit and veggies are just as nutritious as fresh, but they can come with some unwelcome add-ons.

- Check labels to find options with the lowest amounts of salt and added sugars.

- Choose fruits and vegetables packed in their own juice or water and prepared without heavy syrups or sauces.

- Drain and rinse canned produce.

Eat Colorful Fruits and Vegetables Every Day

Everyone knows you need to eat a few servings of fruits and veggies, but do you know what a serving means?

- One whole medium-size fruit (like an apple, orange, or banana) is a serving.

- Get a whole serving of most fruits and veggies with just a half cup of fresh, frozen, or canned produce.

- One cup of raw leafy veggies provides you with a full serving.

Eat with the Seasons

Seasonal fruits and veggies can make adding color more interesting. Be on the lookout for new produce when the seasons change.

- Shop your local farmers' market to find seasonal fruits and vegetables.

- Join a community garden to add diverse color year-round.

- Grow your own fruit and veggie garden.

Eat a Rainbow

Eat healthier one plate at a time by adding a little color to every meal and snack of the day.

- Look at your plate as a whole each time you eat. If it's looking too beige, add a serving of fruits and veggies.

- Add color to family favorites such as mac and cheese, pasta, and rice by tossing in a handful of veggies.

- Adding color isn't all or nothing; start small, then add more as time goes by.

Go Meatless

Salad isn't the only way to be an herbivore. With colorful substitutions, you won't even miss the meat.

- Replace ground beef in any recipe with finely diced mushrooms.

- Choose a vegetarian meal at least once a week, such as Meatless Mondays.

- Omit the meat and double the veggies in a recipe.

MOVE MORE.

A good starting goal is at least 150 minutes a week, but if you don't want to sweat the numbers, just move more. Find forms of exercise you like and will stick with, and build more opportunities to be active into your routine.

Don't Skip Out on the Warm-Up

Warming up is a critical part of having a safe and efficient workout. Give your body a few minutes of prep time to increase flexibility and prevent injury.

- Five to ten minutes is a good rule of thumb for a sufficient warm-up. The more intense the activity, the longer the warm-up should be.

- Warm up your whole body—not just the muscles you plan on using.

Start Walking

If you're looking for an easy way to add activity to your day, walking could be right up your alley. It's simple, effective, and you can do it almost anywhere.

- Just start walking. Begin with a few minutes each day and add more from there as you get into better shape.

- Find ways to make it fun, whether that's changing your route, inviting a friend, or listening to music.

Gingered Pork with Plums,
page 113

- If you're too busy to carve out time for a longer walk, split it up into shorter sessions that work for you.

Refuel and Hydrate for Optimal Exercise

To stay healthy and get the most out of your workouts, your body needs fuel and fluids before, during, and after your sweat session.

- Hydrate with water and fuel up with healthy carbs up to two hours before working out.

- Take small, frequent sips of water during your workout.

- Refuel after your workout with lean protein, healthy carbs, and plenty of water.

Make Time for Activity

Getting more fit can be as simple as adding at least 22 minutes of activity to each day. Carving out time isn't always easy, but it is worth it.

- Break it up into 10- to 15-minute segments at times that are convenient for you.

- Go for a brisk walk during your lunch break.

- Take the stairs as often as possible for an extra boost.

Get the Whole Family Moving

Adding exercise is easier when it's a shared activity. Bring your family with you for more accountability, time together, and fun.

- Dance your way to fitness with a parents' night out or a fun family dance party.

- Put away the screens and take a walk in your local park.

- Unleash your inner child with fun games such as chase, tag, and kid-friendly obstacle courses.

Recover Quicker with a Cool-Down

Cooling down after a workout can help your body reset so you can avoid dizziness, reduce lactic acid buildup, and recover a little bit easier.

- Gradually reduce your heart rate by walking for about 5 minutes.

- When your muscles are still warm is the best time to stretch.

- Breathing deeply during your cool-down can also help you relax.

BE WELL.

Along with eating smart and being active, real health also includes getting enough sleep, practicing mindfulness, managing stress, keeping mind and body fit, connecting socially, and more.

Rest and Relaxation for the Win

Relaxation is a skill that can be developed. You can take a class to learn new techniques or practice on your own, but the most important thing is to keep it up.

- Practice deep breathing techniques throughout the day by inhaling through your nose and exhaling through your mouth slowly and deliberately.

- Pick up a meditative hobby like walking, painting, gardening, or birdwatching.

- Take up tai chi, qi gong, yoga, or guided meditation with an instructor to develop your technique.

Take It Slow

When you're feeling anxious, stressed out, or angry, take a step back to gather your thoughts and look at the situation objectively.

- In high-anxiety situations, give yourself some space—take a walk and come back later when tensions subside.

- When you're feeling angry or upset with someone, count to ten and take a few deep breaths before you react.

- Take preventive measures to avoid stress, like leaving a few minutes earlier to avoid being late.

Losing Weight and Keeping It Off

- Long-term weight loss and maintenance is all about lifestyle and making healthier choices regularly.

- Losing weight is a simple equation: Eat fewer calories than you burn, and you'll see a difference over time.

- Focus on portion control and eating healthy while increasing calories burned with regular activity such as walking.

- Don't fall into the trap of "cheat days." For long-term results, develop a pattern of healthy eating and indulge sensibly on occasion.

Kick Stress to the Curb

How much stress you have in your life as well as how you react to it can play an important role in your overall well-being. Keep stress at bay with positive coping techniques.

- Focus on healthy outlets for your stress, such as taking a walk, journaling, volunteering, or taking up a hobby.

- Add regular exercise and mediation to your routine to help you stay more relaxed under pressure.

- Be sure to get enough sleep and take everything one step at a time, especially when you feel rushed or overworked.

Make Self-Care a Priority

- Too often we put our own needs aside to get things done for family, work, and other responsibilities. To be your best you, it's important to add a healthy dose of self-care.

- Add calming activities to your day, such as lunchtime walks and yoga, to rejuvenate and refresh.

- Take time out for you; use your vacation days, whether it's to go on a big trip or just hang out at home for a staycation.

- Don't overlook your emotional and mental health; get help if you need it to manage stress, anxiety, depression, or grief.

Sleep Your Way to Whole Body Health

- Sleep could be the key to unlocking a healthier you. Amount and quality of sleep can influence your eating habits, mood, memory, and more.

- Proper rest allows you to recharge your batteries, so that you're less likely to crave sugary, fatty foods that provide quick energy.

- How much rest you need is personal, but many people require seven to nine hours of quality sleep each night.

- Be more active, limit caffeine (especially before bed), and establish a bedtime routine to get on track to better sleep.

For more tips, tricks, and recipes, join the movement at **heart.org/HealthyForGood**.

About the Recipes

To help you plan meals and determine how a certain recipe fits into your overall diet, we have provided a nutrition analysis for each recipe in this book. The following guidelines give important details about how the analyses were calculated and products that were used in the recipes. We have made every effort to provide accurate information. Because of the many variables involved in analyzing foods, however, the serving sizes and nutritional values given should be considered approximate.

- Each analysis is for a single serving.

- Garnishes or optional ingredients are not included unless they significantly increase fat, sodium, cholesterol, or sugar content.

- Serving sizes are approximate.

- When more than one ingredient option is listed, the first one is analyzed. When a range of ingredients is given, the average is analyzed.

- Values other than fats are rounded to the nearest whole number. Fat values are rounded to the nearest half gram. Because of the rounding, values for saturated, trans, monounsaturated, and polyunsaturated fats may not add up to the amount shown for total fat value.

- We specify canola, corn, and olive oils in these recipes, but you can also use other unsaturated (nontropical) oils, such as safflower and sunflower.

- Meats are analyzed as lean, with all visible fat discarded.

- If alcohol is used in a cooked dish, we estimate that most of the alcohol calories evaporate as the food cooks.

- If a recipe in this book calls for commercial products, wherever possible we use and analyze those without added salt (for example, no-salt-added canned beans). If only a regular commercial product is available, we use the brand with the lowest sodium available. (Note that in some cases we call for no-salt-added and lower-sodium products and then add table salt sparingly for flavor. The result still has far less sodium than the full-sodium product would.)

Chickpea Tabbouleh Salad,
page 124

- If this book includes a recipe that can be used in another recipe—for example Chicken Stock (page 39) used in Tomato-Basil Soup with Barley (page 47)—we use the data for our homemade version (rather than store-bought) in the analysis; and the recipe will be cross-referenced.

- Because product labeling in the marketplace can vary and change quickly, we use the generic terms "fat-free" and "low-fat" throughout to avoid confusion.

- We use the abbreviations "g" for gram and "mg" for milligram throughout.

Appetizers & Snacks

Mediterranean Eggplant Dip 29
{Baba Ghanoush}

Creamy Hummus 32

Italian White Bean Dip 33

BBQ Chicken Bites 34

Devilish Eggs 35

Sweet Potato Nachos 36

MEDITERRANEAN EGGPLANT DIP
{Baba Ghanoush}

Do you love getting eggplant dip when you're out at a restaurant? This dip is so easy to make you can now prepare it whenever you want it at home. It's delicious served with fresh vegetables. For a unique flair, serve spoonfuls on endive leaves and garnish with a sprinkling of paprika.

Total prep, cooking, and pressure release time: 21 minutes

1 tablespoon olive oil

1 medium eggplant (about 1 pound), peeled and cut into 1-inch cubes

4 medium garlic cloves, minced

½ cup fat-free, low-sodium vegetable broth, such as on page 41

2 tablespoons fresh lemon juice and 2 tablespoons fresh lemon juice, divided use

½ teaspoon paprika (smoked preferred) and (optional) paprika to taste, divided use

2 tablespoons tahini

Carrot sticks, red bell pepper strips, cucumber slices, and endive leaves (optional)

1. Heat the oil in the pressure cooker on sauté. Cook the eggplant for 3 minutes, or until the edges are lightly browned, stirring frequently. Add the garlic and cook for 30 seconds, stirring frequently. Turn off the pressure cooker.

2. Stir in the broth, 2 tablespoons lemon juice, and ½ teaspoon paprika. Secure the lid. Cook on high pressure for 3 minutes. Quickly release the pressure.

3. Reserving the cooking liquid, drain the eggplant. Transfer the eggplant to a food processor. Add the remaining 2 tablespoons lemon juice and the tahini. Process until smooth. Add 1 to 2 teaspoons reserved cooking liquid for a thinner consistency. Lightly sprinkle the dip with the remaining paprika to taste.

4. Serve with carrot sticks, bell pepper strips, cucumber slices, and endive leaves.

SERVES 6; ¼ cup per serving

PER SERVING Calories 75 / Total Fat 5.0 g Saturated Fat 0.5 g Trans Fat 0.0 g Polyunsaturated Fat 1.5 g Monounsaturated Fat 2.5 g / Cholesterol 0 mg / Sodium 14 mg / Carbohydrates 7 g / Fiber 2 g / Sugars 3 g / Protein 2 g / Dietary Exchanges 1 vegetable, 1 fat

Italian White Bean Dip,
page 33

Mediterranean Eggplant Dip,
page 29

Creamy Hummus,
page 32

CREAMY HUMMUS

Dried chickpeas provide authentic flavor in this Middle Eastern classic. Fresh vegetables are a good choice for dipping accompaniments. This hummus is equally delicious as a spread for heart-healthy crackers or an open-face sandwich.

Total prep, cooking, and pressure release time: 1 hour 23 minutes

4 cups water

1 cup dried chickpeas, sorted for stones and shriveled peas, rinsed, and drained

3 tablespoons tahini

3 tablespoons fresh lemon juice

2 medium garlic cloves

1 teaspoon ground cumin

½ teaspoon paprika

½ teaspoon salt

3 tablespoons olive oil (extra virgin preferred)

Sliced cucumbers, celery sticks, and cherry tomatoes, for serving (optional)

1. Combine the water and chickpeas in the pressure cooker. Secure the lid. Cook on high pressure for 45 minutes. Allow the pressure to release naturally for 15 minutes, then quickly release any remaining pressure.

2. Reserving the cooking liquid, drain the chickpeas. Rinse the chickpeas under cold water and drain.

3. Transfer the chickpeas to a food processor. Add the tahini, lemon juice, garlic, cumin, paprika, and salt. Process until smooth. With the machine running, add the oil in a steady stream. Drizzle ¼ cup of the reserved chickpea cooking liquid into the processor and puree until the hummus is smooth and creamy. If necessary, add more chickpea cooking liquid until the hummus is the desired consistency.

4. Serve with sliced cucumbers, celery sticks, and cherry tomatoes.

COOK'S TIP ON TAHINI: Tahini is a thick paste made of sesame seeds and is popular in Middle Eastern cooking. Look for it in the ethnic foods aisle of the supermarket.

SERVES 10; ¼ cup per serving

PER SERVING Calories 133 / Total Fat 7.5 g Saturated Fat 1.0 g Trans Fat 0.0 g Polyunsaturated Fat 2.0 g Monounsaturated Fat 4.0 g / Cholesterol 0 mg / Sodium 124 mg / Carbohydrates 13 g / Fiber 3 g / Sugars 2 g / Protein 5 g / Dietary Exchanges 1 starch, 1½ fat

ITALIAN WHITE BEAN DIP

No need for a passport when enjoying this dip. Just imagine sitting at an outdoor café in a quaint Italian town and savoring this creamy, herbed bean dip.

Total prep, cooking, and pressure release time: 1 hour 20 minutes

4 cups water

1 cup dried Great Northern beans, sorted for stones and shriveled beans, rinsed, and drained

2 medium garlic cloves, halved

1 sprig of fresh rosemary (about 3 inches long) and 1 tablespoon minced fresh rosemary, divided use

1 sprig of fresh thyme (about 2 inches long) and 1 tablespoon minced fresh thyme, divided use

2 medium fresh sage leaves and 1 tablespoon minced fresh sage, divided use

1 tablespoon olive oil (extra virgin preferred)

¼ teaspoon pepper

Sprigs of fresh rosemary and sage for garnish (optional)

Bell peppers (assorted colors), cut into strips about ¾ inch wide (optional)

Radishes, trimmed and halved (optional)

Zucchini or cucumber slices (optional)

1. Combine the water and beans in the pressure cooker. Add the garlic, sprigs of rosemary and thyme, and the sage leaves. Secure the lid. Cook on high pressure for 40 minutes. Allow the pressure to release naturally for 15 minutes, then quickly release any remaining pressure.

2. Reserving the cooking liquid, drain the beans. Rinse the beans under cold water and drain. Discard the sprigs of rosemary and thyme and the sage leaves.

3. Transfer the beans to a food processor. Add ¼ cup of the reserved cooking liquid, the oil, pepper, and the remaining 1 tablespoon each minced rosemary, thyme, and sage. Process until smooth.

4. Add an additional ¼ cup reserved cooking liquid for a thinner consistency. Process until smooth.

5. Transfer the bean dip to a serving bowl. Garnish with the fresh herbs. Serve with bell pepper strips, radish halves, and zucchini or cucumber slices.

SERVES 8; ¼ cup per serving

PER SERVING Calories 84 / Total Fat 2.0 g Saturated Fat 0.5 g Trans Fat 0.0 g Polyunsaturated Fat 0.5 g Monounsaturated Fat 1.0 g / Cholesterol 0 mg / Sodium 3 mg / Carbohydrates 12 g / Fiber 4 g / Sugars 0 g / Protein 5 g / Dietary Exchanges 1 starch

BBQ CHICKEN BITES

Prepare these crave-worthy glazed chicken bites for snacking while you're watching the big game. A healthier version of traditional chicken wings, this dish is definitely a winner!

Total prep, cooking, and pressure release time: 17 minutes

1½ cups water

1 teaspoon paprika

8 ounces chicken breast tenders, all visible fat discarded, halved crosswise

2 tablespoons honey

2 tablespoons barbecue sauce (lowest sodium available)

1 tablespoon soy sauce (lowest sodium available)

1. Place the steaming rack in the pressure cooker. Pour in the water. Sprinkle the paprika over the chicken. Place the chicken on the steaming rack. Secure the lid. Cook on high pressure for 5 minutes. Quickly release the pressure.

2. Preheat the broiler. Line a large baking sheet with aluminum foil.

3. In a medium bowl, whisk together the honey, barbecue sauce, and soy sauce. Dip the chicken pieces in the sauce and transfer to the baking sheet. Broil for 1 to 2 minutes per side, or until crisp and charred (watch carefully to avoid burning).

COOK'S TIP: This recipe can easily be doubled and served as a main dish with a dark green, leafy salad.

SERVES 6; 2 pieces per serving

PER SERVING Calories 77 / Total Fat 1.0 g Saturated Fat 0.0 g Trans Fat 0.0 g Polyunsaturated Fat 0.0 g Monounsaturated Fat 0.5 g / Cholesterol 24 mg / Sodium 144 mg / Carbohydrates 9 g / Fiber 0 g / Sugars 8 g / Protein 8 g / Dietary Exchanges ½ other carbohydrate, 1 lean meat

DEVILISH EGGS

Deviled eggs are excellent to kick off a party or to take on a picnic, and this lighter take on the classic is downright heavenly.

Total prep, cooking, and pressure release time: 20 minutes

1 cup water

6 large eggs

3 tablespoons light mayonnaise

2 teaspoons cider vinegar

1 teaspoon Dijon mustard (lowest sodium available)

Thinly sliced fresh chives or paprika for garnish (optional)

1. Fill a large bowl with ice water.

2. Place the steaming rack in the pressure cooker. Pour in the 1 cup water. Place the eggs on the rack. Secure the lid. Cook on high pressure for 7 minutes. Quickly release the pressure. Using tongs, transfer the eggs to the ice water.

3. Let the eggs stand for 2 to 3 minutes. Remove from the water. Peel the eggs.

4. Halve the eggs lengthwise. Discard one yolk. Put the remaining yolks in a bowl. Add the mayonnaise, vinegar, and mustard. Using the tines of a fork, mash the egg yolk mixture until smooth. Spoon into the egg white halves. Sprinkle with the chives or paprika.

SERVES 6; 2 halves per serving

PER SERVING Calories 81 / Total Fat 6.0 g Saturated Fat 1.5 g Trans Fat 0.0 g Polyunsaturated Fat 2.0 g Monounsaturated Fat 2.0 g / Cholesterol 158 mg / Sodium 150 mg / Carbohydrates 1 g / Fiber 0 g / Sugars 0 g / Protein 6 g / Dietary Exchanges 1 lean meat, ½ fat

SWEET POTATO NACHOS

This sweet potato dish is filled with the flavors of nachos. It's so delicious that you'll be tempted to make it often.

Total prep, cooking, and pressure release time: 27 minutes

1 cup fat-free, low-sodium chicken broth or Chicken Stock, such as on page 39

1 teaspoon chili powder

½ teaspoon ground cumin

2 medium unpeeled sweet potatoes, cut crosswise into slices ⅜ to ½ inch thick

1 cup canned no-salt-added black beans, rinsed and drained

¼ cup chopped red bell pepper

2 medium green onions, chopped

½ cup shredded low-fat Cheddar cheese

¼ cup salsa (lowest sodium available)

1 small tomato, seeded and chopped

2 tablespoons fat-free sour cream

1. Pour the broth into the pressure cooker. Stir in the chili powder and cumin. Place the steaming rack in the cooker.

2. Arrange the sweet potato slices on the rack. Secure the lid. Cook on high pressure for 8 minutes. Quickly release the pressure.

3. Spoon the beans over the sweet potatoes. Top with the bell pepper and green onions. Cook, covered, on the steam setting for 3 minutes. Turn off the pressure cooker.

4. Sprinkle the Cheddar over the beans. Let stand, covered, for 1 minute, or until the Cheddar is melted.

5. Using a spatula, carefully transfer the sweet potatoes and toppings to a platter. Top with the salsa and tomato. Dollop with the sour cream.

COOK'S TIP: If you have one, use a steaming rack with a handle so you can lift the cooked sweet potatoes with toppings out of the cooker. You can more easily slide everything from the rack onto a platter. If you don't have a rack with a handle, use a pancake turner or large spoon to make the transfer.

SERVES 4; ½ sweet potato and ½ cup vegetable and bean topping per serving

PER SERVING Calories 175 / Total Fat 1.0 g Saturated Fat 0.5 g Trans Fat 0.0 g Polyunsaturated Fat 0.0 g Monounsaturated Fat 0.5 g / Cholesterol 4 mg / Sodium 227 mg / Carbohydrates 31 g / Fiber 6 g / Sugars 9 g / Protein 10 g / Dietary Exchanges 2 starch, 1 lean meat

Soups

CHICKEN STOCK

Chicken stock is a basic kitchen ingredient and when it's this easy to make, you can make your own to have on hand anytime you want it.

Total prep, cooking, and pressure release time: 1 hour 40 minutes

2 pounds bone-in chicken pieces with skin, all visible fat discarded

1 medium carrot, cut into 2-inch strips

1 small onion, quartered

1 medium rib of celery, leaves discarded, cut into 2-inch pieces

4 or 5 whole black peppercorns or ½ teaspoon black pepper (coarsely ground preferred)

¼ teaspoon salt

2 sprigs of fresh Italian (flat-leaf) parsley (about 2 inches long)

2 sprigs of fresh thyme (about 2 inches long)

6 cups water

1. Combine all the ingredients in the pressure cooker. Secure the lid. Cook on high pressure for 45 minutes. Allow the pressure to release naturally.

2. Pour the stock through a fine-mesh sieve into a deep bowl. Discard the solids. Cover and refrigerate the stock for 8 hours.

3. Using a spoon, skim off and discard any fat from the top of the stock. Cover and refrigerate the stock for up to one to two days, or freeze.

COOK'S TIP: Bones add flavor to the stock, and bony pieces, such as chicken backs and wings, make for an even more delicious stock.

COOK'S TIP ON STOCK: Store the stock in measured portions for convenient use. One way to do this is to use a muffin pan. First, check the size of the wells by pouring a measured amount of water into a well. Many muffin pans comfortably hold ⅓ or ½ cup water. Discard the water. Use that measure as a guide to ladle the stock into each well. Freeze the stock until firm. Invert the pan and, if necessary, quickly run water over the back of the pan to dislodge the cubes of stock. Place the frozen stock cubes in a resealable freezer bag. Label and date the bag, including the volume of the cubes. Then, when you need stock, just add a frozen cube, or several to equal the amount of stock needed, to your recipe. For optimal flavor, plan to use frozen stock within one to two months.

MAKES 7 CUPS

PER SERVING Calories 10 / Total Fat 0.0 g Saturated Fat 0.0 g Trans Fat 0.0 g Polyunsaturated Fat 0.0 g Monounsaturated Fat 0.0 g / Cholesterol 0 mg / Sodium 108 mg / Carbohydrates 1 g / Fiber 0 g / Sugars 0 g / Protein 2 g / Dietary Exchanges Free

BEEF STOCK

Because the flavor of homemade stock is unsurpassed, chefs have long used it in their recipes and you can easily do the same in your kitchen. Plan to make the stock ahead so you can easily skim the fat from the chilled stock.

Total prep, cooking, and pressure release time: 2 hours 35 minutes

2 teaspoons canola or corn oil

3 pounds meaty beef bones, such as oxtails, ribs, or marrow bones, all visible fat discarded, patted dry with paper towels

1 medium onion, quartered

2 medium carrots, quartered

2 medium ribs of celery, leaves discarded, quartered

3 medium garlic cloves, halved

1 sprig of fresh thyme (about 2 inches long)

1 medium dried bay leaf

1 tablespoon red wine vinegar

6 cups water

1. Heat the oil in the pressure cooker on sauté. Cook about half the bones until well browned, turning to brown all over. Don't crowd the bones. Transfer the bones to a plate. Repeat with the remaining bones. Drain well. Turn off the pressure cooker.

2. Place the browned bones in the pressure cooker. Add the onion, carrots, celery, garlic, thyme, bay leaf, and vinegar. Pour in the water. Secure the lid. Cook on high pressure for 1 hour 30 minutes. Allow the pressure to release naturally.

3. Pour the stock through a fine-mesh sieve into a deep bowl. Discard the solids. Cover and refrigerate for 8 hours.

4. Using a spoon, skim off and discard any fat from the top of the stock. Cover and refrigerate for up to one to two days, or freeze.

COOK'S TIP ON STOCK OR BROTH: Frequently, the terms broth and stock are used interchangeably, but technically there is a difference. Both are the result of cooking meat, chicken, or vegetables in water. But stock must be made from bones; the gelatin derived from the bones creates a rich mouthfeel that differentiates stock from broth. Stock is designed for use as an ingredient in other dishes, but broth is seasoned so you can serve it as a light soup. They are very similar, however. For the recipes in this book, feel free to use your own homemade broths or stocks in place of a purchased product.

MAKES 6 CUPS

PER SERVING Calories 10 / Total Fat 0.0 g Saturated Fat 0.0 g Trans Fat 0.0 g Polyunsaturated Fat 0.0 g Monounsaturated Fat 0.0 g / Cholesterol 0 mg / Sodium 30 mg / Carbohydrates 1 g / Fiber 0 g / Sugars 0 g / Protein 2 g / Dietary Exchanges Free

VEGETABLE BROTH

Making your own low-sodium vegetable broth has never been easier. Just combine vegetables and herbs and let the pressure cooker do all the work. You'll discard the cooked vegetables since they've already given all their flavor to this delicious broth.

Total prep, cooking, and pressure release time: 1 hour 27 minutes

1 medium onion, coarsely chopped

2 medium ribs of celery, leaves discarded, cut into 1-inch pieces

2 medium carrots, cut into 1-inch strips

1 medium leek, trimmed, halved, and cut into 1-inch pieces

1 cup button mushrooms, quartered

½ teaspoon dried thyme, crumbled

2 sprigs of fresh Italian (flat-leaf) parsley (about 2 inches long)

1 medium dried bay leaf

10 whole black peppercorns

¼ teaspoon salt

7 cups water

1. Combine all the ingredients in the pressure cooker. Secure the lid. Cook on high pressure for 30 minutes. Allow the pressure to release naturally.

2. Pour the broth through a fine-mesh sieve into a deep bowl. Discard the solids. Cover and refrigerate for up to one to two days, or freeze.

COOK'S TIP ON MAKING STOCK OR BROTH IN A PRESSURE COOKER: Let the pressure cooker do all the work and make flavorful rich stocks and broths. Fill the pressure cooker, typically about two-thirds full. Don't exceed the max fill line. Allow the pressure to release naturally. Depending on your model, use either the high-pressure setting or the soup setting.

COOK'S TIP ON CELERY LEAVES: You can eat and enjoy both the celery ribs and leaves in many dishes, but the leaves are more strongly flavored than the ribs and can be somewhat bitter. The leaves are discarded when making stock and some other dishes due to their stronger flavor. The bitterness can be especially evident in stock or broth because of the longer cooking time. It's your choice when making a salad and many other dishes. If you enjoy the flavor of celery leaves, by all means use them. If making a stock or broth, though, be sure to remove and discard celery leaves.

MAKES 7 CUPS

PER SERVING Calories 5 / Total Fat 0.0 g Saturated Fat 0.0 g Trans Fat 0.0 g Polyunsaturated Fat 0.0 g Monounsaturated Fat 0.0 g / Cholesterol 0 mg / Sodium 93 mg / Carbohydrates 1 g / Fiber 0 g / Sugars 0 g / Protein 0 g / Dietary Exchanges Free

BUTTERNUT SQUASH SOUP

This golden soup soothes and comforts after a busy day. Many grocery stores now sell the squash already peeled and cubed, so preparation is even easier.

Total prep, cooking, and pressure release time: 1 hour

2 teaspoons canola or corn oil

2 medium shallots, chopped

1 medium butternut squash, peeled and cubed (about 3 cups)

3 cups fat-free, low-sodium vegetable broth, such as on page 41

2 tablespoons minced peeled gingerroot

¼ teaspoon salt

¼ teaspoon pepper (coarsely ground preferred)

⅓ cup fat-free half-and-half

¼ teaspoon freshly grated or ground nutmeg

1. Heat the oil in the pressure cooker on sauté. Cook the shallots for 3 minutes, or until soft, stirring frequently. Turn off the pressure cooker.

2. Stir in the squash, broth, gingerroot, salt, and pepper. Secure the lid. Cook on high pressure for 20 minutes. Allow the pressure to release naturally for 10 minutes, then quickly release any remaining pressure. Turn off the pressure cooker. Remove the pressure cooker lid.

3. Allow the soup to cool slightly. Working in batches, transfer the soup to a blender (vent the blender lid) and puree until smooth. (Use caution as the soup and steam are hot and vent the blender lid away from you.) Return the soup to the pressure cooker.

4. Stir in the half-and-half. Cook on the sauté setting for 2 to 3 minutes, or until heated through, stirring frequently. Ladle the soup into bowls. Sprinkle with the nutmeg.

COOK'S TIP: Top this soup with other garnishes, such as toasted pumpkin seeds or peeled, diced apple.

COOK'S TIP ON BUTTERNUT SQUASH: To make the squash easier to peel and cut, pierce the squash in several places with the tip of a sharp knife. Microwave on 100 percent power (high) for 1 to 2 minutes, then let stand for 3 minutes. Using a heavy knife, carefully cut off the stem end and slice through the squash. Scoop out and discard the seeds.

SERVES 6; 1 cup per serving

PER SERVING Calories 64 / Total Fat 1.5 g Saturated Fat 0.0 g Trans Fat 0.0 g Polyunsaturated Fat 0.5 g Monounsaturated Fat 1.0 g / Cholesterol 0 mg / Sodium 126 mg / Carbohydrates 12 g / Fiber 2 g / Sugars 3 g / Protein 2 g / Dietary Exchanges 1 starch

FRESH CORN SOUP

If summer could taste like a spoonful of soup, this would be it. It's rich and chock-full of corn and fresh herbs along with a garnish of a summer-ripe tomato. But don't wait until summer to make this delicious soup. Go ahead and make it year-round, using frozen ears of corn. If tomatoes aren't in season, omit the tomato as the soup tastes great even without it. For added color, use chopped grape or cherry tomatoes as a garnish.

Total prep, cooking, and pressure release time: 45 minutes

2 teaspoons olive oil

⅓ cup chopped onion

1 medium garlic clove, minced

4 medium ears of corn (about 5 inches long), husks and silk discarded

3¼ cups fat-free, low-sodium vegetable broth, such as on page 41

1 tablespoon minced fresh thyme leaves

½ teaspoon pepper (coarsely ground preferred)

1 small tomato, seeded and finely chopped

2 tablespoons minced fresh basil

1. Heat the oil in the pressure cooker on sauté. Cook the onion for 3 minutes, or until soft, stirring frequently. Add the garlic. Cook for 30 seconds, stirring frequently. Turn off the pressure cooker.

2. Put the corn in the pressure cooker with the onion and garlic. Add the broth, thyme, and pepper. Secure the lid. Cook on high pressure for 10 minutes. Allow the pressure to release naturally for 5 minutes, then quickly release any remaining pressure. Turn off the pressure cooker.

3. Using tongs, lift the corn out of the pressure cooker, leaving the liquid. Set the corn aside to cool slightly. When cool enough to handle, cut the corn from the cobs. Set aside ⅔ cup kernels. Stir the remaining kernels into the soup.

4. Allow the soup to cool slightly. Working in batches, transfer the soup to a blender (vent the blender lid) and process until smooth. (Use caution as the soup and steam are hot and vent the blender lid away from you.) Return the soup to the pressure cooker. Stir in the reserved corn kernels. Set on sauté and heat until simmering, stirring frequently.

5. Ladle the soup into bowls. Garnish with the tomato and basil.

COOK'S TIP ON PUREEING SOUP: When blending hot soup (or any hot liquid), allow it to cool slightly, then carefully ladle part of the soup into the blender. Work in batches so as not to overfill the blender. Always vent the lid away from you (or remove the center cap) so the steam can safely escape.

SERVES 6; 1 cup per serving

PER SERVING Calories 85 / Total Fat 2.5 g Saturated Fat 0.5 g Trans Fat 0.0 g Polyunsaturated Fat 0.5 g Monounsaturated Fat 1.5 g / Cholesterol 0 mg / Sodium 24 mg / Carbohydrates 15 g / Fiber 2 g / Sugars 5 g / Protein 3 g / Dietary Exchanges 1 starch, ½ fat

VEGETABLE SOUP with Chard

The vegetables in this recipe come together to make a delicious soup, but you can tweak the flavors to fit your preferences, so add herbs or substitute kale or spinach for the chard if that's what you have on hand.

Total prep, cooking, and pressure release time: 46 minutes

2 teaspoons olive oil

½ medium onion, chopped

2 medium garlic cloves, minced

4 cups fat-free, low-sodium vegetable broth, such as on page 41

2 medium carrots, chopped

1 medium rib of celery, leaves discarded, chopped

1 medium leek, halved lengthwise and chopped

1 medium potato, peeled and cut into ½-inch cubes

2 tablespoons minced fresh Italian (flat-leaf) parsley

½ teaspoon dried thyme, crumbled

½ teaspoon pepper

⅛ teaspoon salt

2 cups coarsely chopped Swiss chard leaves, tough stems discarded

1 teaspoon white wine vinegar

1. Heat the oil in the pressure cooker on sauté. Cook the onions for 3 minutes, or until soft, stirring frequently. Add the garlic. Cook for 30 seconds, stirring frequently. Turn off the pressure cooker.

2. Add the broth, carrots, celery, leek, potato, parsley, thyme, pepper, and salt. Secure the lid. Cook on high pressure for 10 minutes. Allow the pressure to release naturally for 10 minutes, then quickly release any remaining pressure. Remove the pressure cooker lid.

3. Set on sauté and heat the soup until simmering. Stir in the chard and vinegar. Cook for 3 minutes, or until the chard is tender, stirring occasionally.

COOK'S TIP ON LEEKS: Trim and discard the root end and the tougher dark green leaves. For easy washing, halve the leek lengthwise and separate the leaves. Wash the leek under running water or submerge it in water, washing well between the leaves to remove any trapped dirt.

COOK'S TIP ON CHARD: Several varieties of Swiss chard are available and the color of the leaves and stems varies, but dark green leaves and a reddish stem are common. Submerge the leaves in water, swish well, and rinse until all the grit is gone. Tear the leaves off the stem, then coarsely chop the leaves.

SERVES 6; 1 cup per serving

PER SERVING Calories 76 / Total Fat 1.5 g Saturated Fat 0.0 g Trans Fat 0.0 g Polyunsaturated Fat 0.0 g Monounsaturated Fat 1.0 g / Cholesterol 0 mg / Sodium 118 mg / Carbohydrates 14 g / Fiber 2 g / Sugars 3 g / Protein 2 g / Dietary Exchanges ½ starch, 1 vegetable

TOMATO-BASIL SOUP
with Barley

This creamy version of tomato soup is hearty and filling thanks to the addition of a whole grain.

Total prep, cooking, and pressure release time: 30 minutes

2 teaspoons olive oil

1 medium onion, chopped

2 medium carrots, finely chopped

2 medium garlic cloves, minced

1 28-ounce can no-salt-added crushed tomatoes, undrained

1 14.5-ounce can fat-free, low-sodium chicken broth or 1¾ cups Chicken Stock, such as on page 39

½ cup uncooked quick-cooking (10-minute) barley

1 teaspoon dried basil, crumbled

¼ teaspoon pepper (coarsely ground preferred)

2 tablespoons fat-free sour cream

1. Heat the oil in the pressure cooker on sauté. Cook the onion and carrots for 5 minutes, or until the onion is soft and the carrots are tender, stirring frequently. Add the garlic. Cook for 30 seconds, stirring frequently.

2. Stir in the tomatoes with liquid, broth, barley, basil, and pepper. Secure the lid. Cook on the soup setting for 5 minutes. Allow the pressure to release naturally for 10 minutes, then quickly release any remaining pressure.

3. Stir in the sour cream until blended. Serve warm.

SERVES 6; 1 cup per serving

PER SERVING Calories 136 / Total Fat 2.0 g Saturated Fat 0.5 g Trans Fat 0.0 g Polyunsaturated Fat 0.5 g Monounsaturated Fat 1.0 g / Cholesterol 1 mg / Sodium 61 mg / Carbohydrates 26 g / Fiber 5 g / Sugars 8 g / Protein 5 g / Dietary Exchanges 1 starch, 3 vegetable

MINESTRONE SOUP

This is a nutrient-filled way to begin your meal. You can add any combination of vegetables that you might have on hand and your favorite variety of beans and pasta. It's a great way to use leftovers in the vegetable bin.

Total prep, cooking, and pressure release time: 1 hour

2 teaspoons olive oil

3 medium carrots, diced

2 medium ribs of celery, leaves discarded, sliced

1 onion, diced

⅔ cup unpeeled chopped zucchini

2 cups water

1 15.5-ounce can no-salt-added dark red kidney beans, rinsed and drained

1 14.5-ounce can no-salt-added diced tomatoes, undrained

1 tablespoon dried Italian seasoning, crumbled

3 medium garlic cloves, minced

16 ounces spinach (about 4 cups tightly packed)

½ cup dried whole-grain pasta

½ cup shredded or grated Parmesan cheese

1. Heat the oil in the pressure cooker on sauté. Cook the carrots, celery, onion, and zucchini for 5 minutes, stirring frequently. Stir in the water, beans, tomatoes with liquid, Italian seasoning, and garlic. Secure the lid. Cook on high pressure (or on the soup setting if available) for 10 minutes. Allow the pressure to release naturally for 15 minutes, then quickly release any remaining pressure. Remove the pressure cooker lid.

2. Set the pressure cooker to sauté. Add the spinach and pasta. Cook for 10 minutes, or until the pasta is al dente, stirring frequently.

3. Ladle the soup into bowls. Sprinkle with the Parmesan before serving.

SERVES 8; scant 1 cup per serving

PER SERVING Calories 147 / Total Fat 3.0 g Saturated Fat 1.0 g Trans Fat 0.0 g Polyunsaturated Fat 0.5 g Monounsaturated Fat 1.5 g / Cholesterol 4 mg / Sodium 168 mg / Carbohydrates 24 g / Fiber 6 g / Sugars 6 g / Protein 9 g / Dietary Exchanges 1 starch, 2 vegetable, ½ lean meat

HOMESTYLE CHICKEN NOODLE SOUP

A bowl of chicken noodle soup always equals comfort. The vegetables add nutrition and an aromatic flavor. This soup can be prepared at a moment's notice and turns mealtime into a warm and satisfying experience.

Total prep, cooking, and pressure release time: 53 minutes

2 teaspoons olive oil

3 medium carrots, thinly sliced

2 medium ribs of celery, leaves discarded, thinly sliced

1 small onion, diced

4 cups fat-free, low-sodium chicken broth or Chicken Stock, such as on page 39

1½ pounds boneless, skinless chicken breasts, all visible fat discarded, cut into bite-size pieces

3 cups water

3 tablespoons fresh Italian (flat-leaf) parsley, minced

½ teaspoon dried thyme, crumbled

¼ teaspoon salt

¼ teaspoon pepper (coarsely ground preferred)

6 ounces dried no-yolk noodles

1. Heat the oil in the pressure cooker on sauté. Cook the carrots, celery, and onion for 3 minutes, or until the carrots and celery are tender and the onion is soft, stirring frequently. Stir in the broth, chicken, water, parsley, thyme, salt, and pepper.

2. Secure the lid. Cook on high pressure for 12 minutes. Allow the pressure to release naturally for 10 minutes, then quickly release any remaining pressure. Remove the pressure cooker lid.

3. Set the pressure cooker to sauté. Heat until the soup comes to a simmer. Stir in the noodles. Cook for 8 to 10 minutes, or until the noodles are tender, stirring frequently.

SERVES 6; 2 cups per serving

PER SERVING Calories 282 / Total Fat 5.0 g Saturated Fat 1.0 g Trans Fat 0.0 g Polyunsaturated Fat 0.5 g Monounsaturated Fat 2.0 g / Cholesterol 73 mg / Sodium 324 mg / Carbohydrates 27 g / Fiber 3 g / Sugars 4 g / Protein 30 g / Dietary Exchanges 1½ starch, 1 vegetable, 3 lean meat

ASIAN PORK NOODLE SOUP

The bowls of freshly cooked noodles in rich pork soup that you'll find at Japanese restaurants are delicious. Now you can enjoy that experience without added salt and fat. Cook the udon noodles just before serving, then ladle the hot soup over them. This will give you the best flavor and texture and help you avoid overcooked or mushy noodles.

Total prep, cooking, and pressure release time: 58 minutes

2 teaspoons canola or corn oil

1 1-pound pork tenderloin, all visible fat discarded, cut into bite-size pieces

1 medium onion, chopped

1½ cups sliced button mushrooms (about 6 ounces)

4 cups fat-free, low-sodium chicken broth or Chicken Stock, such as on page 39

2 cups coarsely chopped kale, tough stems discarded

1 cup water

2 tablespoons minced peeled gingerroot

3 medium garlic cloves, minced

¼ teaspoon crushed red pepper flakes (optional)

½ teaspoon pepper (coarsely ground preferred)

6 ounces dried udon noodles or whole-grain fettuccine or spaghetti

Sliced radishes for garnish (optional)

Sliced green onions for garnish (optional)

1. Heat the oil in the pressure cooker on sauté. Cook the pork for 4 to 6 minutes, or until browned, stirring frequently. Add the onion. Cook for 3 minutes, or until the onion is soft, stirring frequently. Add the mushrooms. Cook for 3 minutes, stirring occasionally.

2. Stir in the broth, kale, water, gingerroot, garlic, and pepper. Secure the lid. Cook on high pressure for 10 minutes. Allow the pressure to release naturally for 10 minutes, then quickly release any remaining pressure.

3. Meanwhile, prepare the noodles using the package directions, omitting the salt.

4. Transfer the noodles to serving bowls. Ladle the soup over the noodles. Garnish with the radishes and green onions.

SERVES 4; 1½ cups per serving

PER SERVING Calories 342 / Total Fat 7.0 g Saturated Fat 1.0 g Trans Fat 0.0 g Polyunsaturated Fat 1.0 g Monounsaturated Fat 2.5 g / Cholesterol 60 mg / Sodium 186 mg / Carbohydrates 38 g / Fiber 4 g / Sugars 4 g / Protein 32 g / Dietary Exchanges 2 starch, 2 vegetable, 3 lean meat

HERBED BEAN SOUP with Kale

Bean soup with kale is lighter than many traditional bean soups, but it's still comforting and rich. Garlic and sage add a depth of flavor to this satisfying combo of beans, carrots, and kale.

Total prep, cooking, and pressure release time: 1 hour 39 minutes

4 cups water

1 cup dried Great Northern beans, sorted for stones and shriveled beans, rinsed, and drained

2 teaspoons canola or corn oil

1 medium onion, chopped

2 large garlic cloves, minced

4 cups fat-free, low-sodium vegetable broth, such as on page 41

2 medium carrots, chopped

1 teaspoon dried rubbed sage

½ teaspoon pepper (coarsely ground preferred)

¼ teaspoon salt

⅛ teaspoon cayenne

2 cups coarsely chopped kale leaves, tough stems discarded

1. Combine the water and beans in the pressure cooker. Secure the lid. Cook on high pressure for 20 minutes. Allow the pressure to release naturally. Drain in a colander.

2. Heat the oil in the pressure cooker on sauté. Cook the onion for 3 minutes, or until soft, stirring frequently. Add the garlic. Cook for 30 seconds, stirring frequently. Turn off the pressure cooker.

3. Stir in the broth, carrots, sage, pepper, salt, cayenne, and beans. Secure the lid. Cook on high pressure for 10 minutes. Allow the pressure to release naturally. Remove the pressure cooker lid.

4. Set on sauté and heat the soup until simmering. Stir in the kale. Cook for 3 minutes, or until the kale is tender, stirring occasionally.

COOK'S TIP ON KALE: Discard any wilted or yellow leaves. Remove the stem and central ribs. Wash the leaves well by submerging them in water and rinsing well until all the grit has been removed. Tear the tender leaves into bite-size pieces. Several varieties of kale are readily available and among them are lacinato (Tuscan) kale, which is a little more delicate and milder in flavor. Packaged pretorn kale and other greens are readily available in the grocery store and make preparation faster and easier.

SERVES 4; 1¾ cups per serving

PER SERVING Calories 209 / Total Fat 3.5 g Saturated Fat 0.5 g Trans Fat 0.0 g Polyunsaturated Fat 1.0 g Monounsaturated Fat 1.5 g / Cholesterol 0 mg / Sodium 217 mg / Carbohydrates 35 g / Fiber 11 g / Sugars 4 g / Protein 13 g / Dietary Exchanges 1½ starch, 2 vegetable, 1 lean meat

PASTA E FAGIOLI SOUP

This Italian soup trounces the restaurant version, hands down.

Total prep, cooking, and pressure release time: 1 hour 18 minutes

2 teaspoons olive oil

8 ounces low-fat bulk Italian turkey sausage

2 cups water and 2 cups water, divided use

½ cup dried red kidney beans, sorted for stones and shriveled beans, rinsed, and drained

1 14.5-ounce can no-salt-added diced tomatoes, undrained

1 14.5-ounce can fat-free, low-sodium chicken broth or 1¾ cups Chicken Stock (page 39)

1 large onion, chopped

2 medium ribs of celery with leaves, chopped

2 medium carrots, chopped

3 medium garlic cloves, minced

1 teaspoon dried basil, crumbled

1 teaspoon dried oregano, crumbled

¼ teaspoon pepper (coarsely ground preferred)

¾ cup dried whole-grain ditalini or other small whole-grain pasta

¼ cup shredded or grated Parmesan cheese (freshly grated preferred)

1. Heat the oil in the pressure cooker on sauté. Cook the sausage for 5 minutes, or until browned on the outside and no longer pink in the center, stirring occasionally to turn and break up the sausage. Transfer to a plate. Set aside.

2. Turn off the pressure cooker for 5 minutes. Using paper towels, wipe the cooker.

3. Combine 2 cups water and the beans in the pressure cooker. Secure the lid. Cook on high pressure for 15 minutes. Allow the pressure to release naturally. Turn off the pressure cooker. Remove the pressure cooker lid. Allow the beans to cool slightly. Drain.

4. Return the beans to the cooker. Add the sausage, the remaining 2 cups water, tomatoes with liquid, broth, onion, celery, carrots, garlic, basil, oregano, and pepper. Secure the lid. Cook on high pressure for 10 minutes. Quickly release the pressure.

5. Remove the pressure cooker lid. Set to sauté. Stir in the pasta. Cook for 5 minutes, or until the pasta is tender. Ladle the soup into bowls. Sprinkle with the Parmesan.

SERVES 4; 2 cups per serving

PER SERVING Calories 338 / Total Fat 8.5 g Saturated Fat 2.5 g Trans Fat 0.0 g Polyunsaturated Fat 2.0 g Monounsaturated Fat 4.0 g / Cholesterol 48 mg / Sodium 478 mg / Carbohydrates 43 g / Fiber 11 g / Sugars 10 g / Protein 22 g / Dietary Exchanges 2 starch, 2 vegetable, 2 lean meat

Seafood

MOROCCAN FISH TAGINE

Morocco, in northwest Africa, is known for delicious foods flavored with cumin, cilantro, and pepper. One of the most famous Moroccan recipes, the tagine, is a stew named for the pottery dish in which it's cooked. The flavors of North Africa and the tagine are captured in this fish stew.

Total prep, cooking, and pressure release time: 24 minutes

2 teaspoons olive oil

1 medium onion, chopped

½ medium red bell pepper, chopped

1 medium fresh jalapeño, seeds and ribs discarded, chopped

3 medium garlic cloves, minced

4 medium carrots, sliced 1 inch thick

2 firm white fish fillets (about 8 ounces each), such as cod or haddock, about 1 inch thick, rinsed and patted dry, cut into 2-inch pieces

1 teaspoon paprika

½ teaspoon ground cumin

¼ teaspoon salt

¼ teaspoon pepper (coarsely ground preferred)

1 14.5-ounce can no-salt-added diced tomatoes, undrained

1 tablespoon fresh lemon juice

2 tablespoons minced fresh cilantro

1. Heat the oil in the pressure cooker on sauté. Cook the onion for 3 minutes, or until soft, stirring frequently. Stir in the bell pepper. Cook for 3 minutes, stirring frequently. Add the jalapeño and garlic. Cook for 30 seconds, stirring frequently. Turn off the pressure cooker.

2. Stir in the carrots and fish. In a small bowl, stir together the paprika, cumin, salt, and pepper. Sprinkle over the fish mixture. Pour the tomatoes with liquid over all. Secure the lid. Cook on high pressure for 3 minutes. Quickly release the pressure.

3. Stir in the lemon juice. Spoon the stew into bowls. Sprinkle each serving with the cilantro.

SERVES 4; 3 ounces fish and 1 cup vegetables per serving

PER SERVING Calories 179 / Total Fat 3.5 g Saturated Fat 0.5 g Trans Fat 0.0 g Polyunsaturated Fat 0.5 g Monounsaturated Fat 2.0 g / Cholesterol 43 mg / Sodium 271 mg / Carbohydrates 17 g / Fiber 4 g / Sugars 10 g / Protein 20 g / Dietary Exchanges 3 vegetable, 3 lean meat

JERK-SEASONED FISH and VEGETABLES with Lime Yogurt

Jerk seasoning, a blend from the Caribbean, adds sweet heat. Start using it and say goodbye to ho-hum dishes. Try this quick, spicy, and captivating fish entrée with its combo of mushrooms, fennel, and asparagus that's served with a tangy sauce.

Total prep, cooking, and pressure release time: 24 minutes

2 teaspoons canola or corn oil

1 medium onion, chopped

1 cup sliced brown (cremini) mushrooms

½ medium red bell pepper, chopped

1 fennel bulb, halved, cored, and thinly sliced

4 firm white fish fillets (about 4 ounces each), such as tilapia, cod, catfish, or snapper, ½ to ¾ inch thick, rinsed and patted dry

4 medium asparagus spears, about ¾ inch in diameter

1 tablespoon salt-free jerk seasoning blend (see Cook's Tip on page 59)

1 cup fat-free, low-sodium vegetable broth, such as on page 41

¼ cup fat-free plain Greek yogurt

½ teaspoon grated lime zest

1 teaspoon fresh lime juice

1. Heat the oil in the pressure cooker on sauté. Cook the onion for 3 minutes, or until soft, stirring frequently. Add the mushrooms and bell pepper. Cook for 3 minutes, stirring frequently. Stir in the fennel. Turn off the pressure cooker. Place the steaming rack over the vegetables. Arrange the fish in a single layer on the rack. Place the asparagus on the fish.

2. Sprinkle the jerk seasoning over the fish and vegetables. Pour the broth around the fish. Secure the lid. Cook on high pressure for 3 minutes. Quickly release the pressure.

3. In a small bowl, whisk together the yogurt, lime zest, and lime juice. Serve the fish and vegetables with the yogurt sauce.

SERVES 4; 3 ounces fish, ⅔ cup vegetables, and 1 tablespoon sauce per serving

PER SERVING Calories 182 / Total Fat 4.5 g Saturated Fat 1.0 g Trans Fat 0.0 g Polyunsaturated Fat 1.0 g Monounsaturated Fat 2.0 g / Cholesterol 57 mg / Sodium 103 mg / Carbohydrates 10 g / Fiber 4 g / Sugars 4 g / Protein 27 g / Dietary Exchanges 2 vegetable, 3 lean meat

COOK'S TIP ON JERK SEASONING: Read the label to be sure it's salt-free. Or, to make your own: Stir together 1 tablespoon onion powder; 1 tablespoon garlic powder; 1 tablespoon dried parsley, crumbled; 1 tablespoon dried minced onion; 2 teaspoons dried thyme, crumbled; 2 teaspoons sugar; 1½ teaspoons cayenne; 1 teaspoon paprika; and 1 teaspoon ground allspice. Reduce the cayenne to 1 teaspoon for a milder flavor or increase it to 2 teaspoons for a spicier flavor. Store the spice mixture, tightly covered, at room temperature for up to six months.

COOK'S TIP ON COOKING FISH IN A PRESSURE COOKER:
The thickness of the fish fillets will affect the cooking time.
Fish fillets that are ¾ to 1 inch thick cook in 4 minutes. If the
fish fillets you're cooking are thinner, cook on high pressure
for 2 or 3 minutes. If you're using thinner fish fillets for this
recipe, slice the summer squash and carrots more thinly so
they cook in the same time as the fish.

HERBED FISH with Vegetables

This pressure-cooked fish is placed on a rack and rests above the liquid, yet cooks quickly and is delicately flavored by fresh parsley and thyme.

Total prep, cooking, and pressure release time: 20 minutes

1 small unpeeled yellow summer squash, cut into 1-inch slices

1 medium carrot, cut into ¾-inch rounds

2 cups fat-free, low-sodium chicken broth or Chicken Stock, such as on page 39

1½ cups water

2 to 3 teaspoons grated lemon zest

3 tablespoons fresh lemon juice

2 sprigs of fresh Italian (flat-leaf) parsley and 2 sprigs of fresh parsley for garnish, divided use

1 sprig of fresh thyme and 1 sprig of fresh thyme for garnish, divided use

1 medium dried bay leaf

4 firm white fish fillets (about 4 ounces each), such as sole, cod, or haddock, ¾ to 1 inch thick

16 ounces spinach

1. Put the squash and carrot in the pressure cooker. Pour the broth and water over the vegetables. Stir in the lemon zest, lemon juice, 2 sprigs of Italian parsley, 1 sprig of thyme, and the bay leaf.

2. Place the steaming rack over the vegetables. (It's fine if the steaming rack rests on the vegetables.) Arrange the fish fillets in a single layer on the rack. (The fish on the rack will be resting above the liquid and won't be submerged.) Secure the lid. Cook on high pressure for 4 minutes. Quickly release the pressure. Remove the pressure cooker lid.

3. Using a spatula or pancake turner, carefully transfer the fish from the rack to a platter. Cover to keep warm. Remove the steaming rack from the cooker. Don't drain off the liquid. Using tongs, discard the parsley, thyme, and bay leaf.

4. Set the pressure cooker to sauté. Heat until simmering. Stir in the spinach. Cook for 3 minutes, or until the spinach is tender, stirring occasionally.

5. Using a slotted spoon, lift the cooked spinach and vegetables out of the liquid. Arrange the vegetables on a platter. Place the fish on the vegetables. Garnish with the remaining 2 sprigs of parsley and 1 sprig of thyme.

SERVES 4; 3 ounces fish and ½ cup vegetables per serving

PER SERVING Calories 150 / Total Fat 2.0 g Saturated Fat 0.5 g Trans Fat 0.0 g Polyunsaturated Fat 0.5 g Monounsaturated Fat 0.5 g / Cholesterol 54 mg / Sodium 227 mg / Carbohydrates 8 g / Fiber 4 g / Sugars 3 g / Protein 26 g / Dietary Exchanges 2 vegetable, 3 lean meat

FRENCH-STYLE FISH
with Tomatoes, Garlic, and Parmesan

The flavors of Southern France inspire this recipe as the fish is topped with tomatoes, garlic, and herbs. The crisp, Parmesan-flavored crumbs are a tasty accent. Sprinkle them over the fish just before serving to ensure they stay crisp.

Total prep, cooking, and pressure release time: 16 minutes

4 lean white fish fillets (about 4 ounces each), such as trout, tilapia, or whiting, about ¾ inch thick, rinsed and patted dry

2 tablespoons minced fresh Italian (flat-leaf) parsley

1 tablespoon minced fresh basil

¼ teaspoon pepper (coarsely ground preferred)

⅛ teaspoon salt

1 14.5-ounce can diced no-salt-added tomatoes, undrained

1 teaspoon olive oil

1 medium garlic clove, minced

3 tablespoons panko (Japanese-style bread crumbs)

3 tablespoons shredded or grated Parmesan cheese

1. Arrange the fish fillets in the pressure cooker. Sprinkle the parsley, basil, pepper, and salt over the fish. Pour the tomatoes with liquid over the fish. Secure the lid. Cook on high pressure for 3 minutes. Quickly release the pressure.

2. Meanwhile, in a small skillet, heat the oil over medium heat, swirling to coat the bottom. Add the garlic. Cook for 30 seconds, stirring frequently. Add the panko. Cook for 2 to 3 minutes, or until the crumbs are toasted and golden brown, stirring frequently. Remove from the heat.

3. Arrange the fish on a serving plate. Stir the Parmesan into the toasted panko. Sprinkle the panko mixture over the fish.

SERVES 4; 3 ounces fish per serving

PER SERVING Calories 200 / Total Fat 6.0 g Saturated Fat 1.5 g Trans Fat 0.0 g Polyunsaturated Fat 1.5 g Monounsaturated Fat 2.5 g / Cholesterol 70 mg / Sodium 191 mg / Carbohydrates 8 g / Fiber 1 g / Sugars 3 g / Protein 26 g / Dietary Exchanges 1 vegetable, 3 lean meat

SALMON
with Cucumber-Dill Sauce

Arctic char, striped bass, swordfish, halibut, or tuna are great choices for use in a pressure cooker. Any type of fish will partner beautifully with the cucumber-dill sauce.

Total prep, cooking, and pressure release time: 19 minutes

⅓ cup fat-free plain Greek yogurt

¼ cup shredded, peeled, and seeded cucumber, patted dry with paper towels

1 teaspoon minced fresh dillweed or ¼ teaspoon dried dillweed, crumbled

¾ teaspoon fresh lemon juice and 1 tablespoon fresh lemon juice, divided use

1 small garlic clove, minced

⅛ teaspoon salt

⅛ teaspoon pepper (coarsely ground preferred)

1¼ cups fat-free, low-sodium chicken broth or Chicken Stock, such as on page 39

¼ cup dry white wine (regular or nonalcoholic)

4 salmon fillets (about 4 ounces each), about 1 inch thick, rinsed and patted dry

¼ teaspoon paprika

1. In a small bowl, stir together the yogurt, cucumber, 1 teaspoon dillweed, ¾ teaspoon lemon juice, the garlic, salt, and pepper.

2. In the pressure cooker, stir together the broth, wine, and the remaining 1 tablespoon lemon juice. Place a steaming rack in the cooker. Arrange the fish fillets in a single layer on the rack. Sprinkle the paprika over the fish. Secure the lid. Cook on high pressure for 4 minutes. Quickly release the pressure.

3. Serve each fish fillet topped with a dollop of the sauce.

COOK'S TIP: Omit the wine and increase the broth to 1½ cups if desired.

SERVES 4; 3 ounces fish and 2 tablespoons sauce per serving

PER SERVING Calories 170 / Total Fat 5.0 g Saturated Fat 1.0 g Trans Fat 0.0 g Polyunsaturated Fat 1.0 g Monounsaturated Fat 1.5 g / Cholesterol 53 mg / Sodium 186 mg / Carbohydrates 2 g / Fiber 0 g / Sugars 1 g / Protein 26 g / Dietary Exchanges 3 lean meat

SALMON EN PAPILLOTE

The name of this dish may not be familiar to you, but it simply means that the fish is cooked enclosed in a cooking parchment packet. With this method, not only are the flavors of the fish and vegetables locked inside, but serving and cleanup are a breeze.

Total prep, cooking, and pressure release time: 32 minutes

2 cups water

1 teaspoon olive oil

4 salmon fillets (about 4 ounces each), rinsed and patted dry

1 small unpeeled zucchini, very thinly sliced

1 medium tomato, seeded and chopped

2 tablespoons minced fresh Italian (flat-leaf) parsley

1 tablespoon minced fresh thyme

1 tablespoon minced fresh rosemary

1 medium garlic clove, minced

½ teaspoon pepper (coarsely ground preferred)

1. Pour the water into the pressure cooker. Place the steaming rack in the pressure cooker.

2. Place 4 sheets of cooking parchment (each about 12 x 16 inches) on the countertop. Drizzle ¼ teaspoon oil onto the center of each sheet. Brush to coat the center of the parchment.

3. Place a fish fillet in the center of each parchment sheet. Arrange the zucchini and tomato on the fish.

4. In a small bowl, stir together the remaining ingredients. Sprinkle the herb mixture over the fish and vegetables. Pull the edges of the parchment over the fish and vegetables. Fold the edges together several times, creasing tightly, to seal the packets securely.

5. Place 2 packets in the center of a sheet (about 18 inches square) of heavy-duty aluminum foil. Gently place the remaining 2 packets on top, perpendicular to the bottom 2 packets. Pull the edges of the foil over all, shaping into a bundle about 8 inches in diameter (to fit in the cooker). Fold the edges together several times, creasing tightly, to seal the foil packet securely.

(CONTINUED)

6. Transfer the foil packet to the rack in the pressure cooker, gently pressing in on the packet so it fits in the cooker and rests well below the max fill line. Secure the lid. Pressure cook on high for 12 minutes. Quickly release the pressure.

7. Carefully lift the foil packet out of the pressure cooker. Transfer to the countertop. Remove the parchment packets from the foil packet. Transfer to serving plates. Or, using the tines of a fork, carefully open the parchment packets away from you (to prevent steam burns) and transfer the fish and vegetables to serving plates.

SERVES 4; 3 ounces fish and ½ cup vegetables per serving

PER SERVING Calories 172 / Total Fat 6.5 g Saturated Fat 1.0 g Trans Fat 0.0 g Polyunsaturated Fat 1.0 g Monounsaturated Fat 2.5 g / Cholesterol 53 mg / Sodium 93 mg / Carbohydrates 3 g / Fiber 1 g / Sugars 1 g / Protein 25 g / Dietary Exchanges 3 lean meat

SALMON with Bok Choy

Are you a fan of bok choy? If it's a new vegetable for you, this is the time to try it. It's now readily available at most grocery stores and local farmers' markets may feature it. This mild vegetable is a perfect accompaniment for salmon.

Total prep, cooking, and pressure release time: 14 minutes

1½ cups fat-free, low-sodium chicken broth or Chicken Stock, such as on page 39

2 tablespoons grated peeled gingerroot

2 medium garlic cloves, minced

1 teaspoon plain rice vinegar

1 bunch bok choy (9 to 10 ounces), cut crosswise into 1-inch slices

4 salmon fillets (about 4 ounces each), about 1 inch thick, rinsed and patted dry

1. In the pressure cooker, stir together the broth, gingerroot, garlic, and vinegar. Stir in the bok choy.

2. Place the steaming rack in the pressure cooker. Place the fish on the rack.

3. Secure the lid. Cook on high pressure for 4 minutes. Quickly release the pressure.

4. Using a spatula or pancake turner, carefully transfer the fish to a platter. Remove the rack. Using a slotted spoon, remove the bok choy from the cooker and arrange around the salmon.

COOK'S TIP: Substitute 2 or 3 bunches of baby bok choy, which is often milder and more tender, for a larger head. Just keep the overall weight of 9 to 10 ounces the same. Trim the bottom of the bok choy. Wash it well to remove any grit. For this recipe, cut the bok choy crosswise, across the stem and leaves, into 1-inch slices.

SERVES 4; 3 ounces fish and ¼ cup bok choy per serving

PER SERVING Calories 156 / Total Fat 5.0 g Saturated Fat 1.0 g Trans Fat 0.0 g Polyunsaturated Fat 1.0 g Monounsaturated Fat 1.5 g / Cholesterol 53 mg / Sodium 131 mg / Carbohydrates 2 g / Fiber 1 g / Sugars 1 g / Protein 25 g / Dietary Exchanges 3 lean meat

SWORDFISH with Herbed Tomatoes

The tangy flavor of the tomato sauce enhances the fish and the flavor of the herbs adds to the sauce. This is delicious served on cooked quinoa or brown rice.

Total prep, cooking, and pressure release time: 15 minutes

2 teaspoons olive oil

1 pound swordfish steaks, about 1 inch thick, rinsed and patted dry

1 14.5-ounce can no-salt-added diced tomatoes, undrained

½ cup fat-free, low-sodium chicken broth or Chicken Stock, such as on page 39

2 tablespoons red wine vinegar

2 teaspoons paprika

3 medium garlic cloves, minced

½ teaspoon dried oregano, crumbled

¼ teaspoon crushed red pepper flakes

2 tablespoons minced fresh Italian (flat-leaf) parsley

1. Heat the oil in the pressure cooker on sauté. Cook the fish steaks on one side for about 2 minutes. Carefully transfer to a large plate. Turn off the pressure cooker.

2. In the pressure cooker, stir together the remaining ingredients except the parsley until well blended. Place the fish steaks in the sauce with the browned side up. Spoon some sauce over the fish. Secure the lid. Cook on high pressure for 3 minutes. Quickly release the pressure.

3. Carefully transfer the fish steaks to a platter. Top with the sauce. Sprinkle with the parsley.

COOK'S TIP: You can substitute another firm, white fish, such as cod or halibut, for the swordfish.

SERVES 4; 3 ounces fish and ½ cup sauce per serving

PER SERVING Calories 195 / Total Fat 9.0 g Saturated Fat 2.0 g Trans Fat 0.0 g Polyunsaturated Fat 1.5 g Monounsaturated Fat 4.5 g / Cholesterol 65 mg / Sodium 102 mg / Carbohydrates 6 g / Fiber 1 g / Sugars 3 g / Protein 21 g / Dietary Exchanges 1 vegetable, 3 lean meat

FISH TACOS with Broccoli Slaw

These fish tacos, packed with crunch, are a great way to get your omega-3s. Dinner will be on the table in less than 20 minutes.

Total prep, cooking, and pressure release time: 16 minutes

1 cup water

4 firm white fish fillets (about 4 ounces each), such as cod or halibut, ¾ to 1 inch thick, rinsed and patted dry

1 teaspoon chili powder

½ teaspoon ground cumin

⅛ teaspoon garlic powder

2 cups broccoli slaw

¼ cup chopped fresh cilantro

1 medium green onion, thinly sliced

3 tablespoons light mayonnaise

2 tablespoons fresh lime juice

4 6-inch corn tortillas

1. Pour the water into the pressure cooker. Place the steaming rack in the pressure cooker. Place the fish on the rack.

2. In a small bowl, stir together the chili powder, cumin, and garlic powder. Sprinkle the mixture over the fish. Secure the lid. Cook on high pressure for 4 minutes. Quickly release the pressure.

3. Meanwhile, in a medium bowl, stir together the broccoli slaw, cilantro, and green onion, tossing gently to combine. Stir in the mayonnaise and lime juice until blended.

4. Heat a small nonstick skillet over medium-high heat. Warm the tortillas, one at a time, turning until heated through. Transfer to a work surface. Place the fish on the tortillas. Top with the slaw. Serve immediately.

COOK'S TIP: Omit the tortillas and serve the fish with the slaw on top.

SERVES 4; 3 ounces fish, ¼ cup slaw, and 1 tortilla per serving

PER SERVING Calories 158 / Total Fat 4.0 g Saturated Fat 0.5 g Trans Fat 0.0 g Polyunsaturated Fat 2.5 g Monounsaturated Fat 1.0 g / Cholesterol 47 mg / Sodium 205 mg / Carbohydrates 11 g / Fiber 3 g / Sugars 1 g / Protein 20 g / Dietary Exchanges ½ starch, 3 lean meat

Fish Tacos with Broccoli Slaw,
page 69

CHEESY TUNA PENNE
with Edamame

You'll enjoy this updated, no-guilt version of the classic tuna noodle casserole that's ready in less than 30 minutes.

Total prep, cooking, and pressure release time: 20 minutes

2 cups water

8 ounces dried whole-grain penne

⅛ teaspoon salt

1¼ cups shredded low-fat Cheddar cheese

¾ cup frozen shelled edamame

2 2.6-ounce vacuum-sealed pouches very low sodium chunk light tuna, packed in water, flaked

½ cup fat-free milk

1. Put the water, pasta, and salt in the pressure cooker. Secure the lid. Cook on high pressure for 4 minutes. Quickly release the pressure. Remove the pressure cooker lid.

2. Set the pressure cooker to sauté. Stir in the Cheddar, edamame, tuna, and milk. Cook for about 3 minutes, stirring occasionally. Turn off the pressure cooker. Let stand for 5 minutes.

COOK'S TIP: Substitute 1 cup frozen green peas for the edamame.

SERVES 4; 1 cup per serving

PER SERVING Calories 345 / Total Fat 5.0 g Saturated Fat 1.5 g Trans Fat 0.0 g Polyunsaturated Fat 1.0 g Monounsaturated Fat 1.5 g / Cholesterol 24 mg / Sodium 553 mg / Carbohydrates 47 g / Fiber 8 g / Sugars 5 g / Protein 31 g / Dietary Exchanges 3 starch, 3 lean meat

SHRIMP JAMBALAYA

Onion, green bell pepper, and celery comprise the "holy trinity" of Cajun cooking, and they're the foundation of this classic dish. This healthy version has such a great, spicy flavor that you won't miss the andouille sausage. Serve with a crisp, dark green salad and enjoy a nutritious meal.

Total prep, cooking, and pressure release time: 55 minutes

2 teaspoons olive oil

3 medium ribs of celery, leaves discarded, sliced

1 large green bell pepper, chopped

1 medium onion, chopped

3 medium garlic cloves, minced

1 14.5-ounce can no-salt-added diced tomatoes, undrained

½ cup uncooked brown rice

½ cup water

1 teaspoon salt-free Cajun or Creole seasoning blend

1 medium dried bay leaf

½ teaspoon dried thyme, crumbled

3 drops red hot-pepper sauce

1 pound raw medium shrimp, peeled and deveined, rinsed, and patted dry

3 tablespoons minced fresh Italian (flat-leaf) parsley

1. Heat the oil in the pressure cooker on sauté. Cook the celery, bell pepper, and onion for 5 minutes, or until the celery and bell pepper are tender and the onion is very soft, stirring frequently. Add the garlic. Cook for 30 seconds, stirring frequently. Turn off the pressure cooker.

2. Add the tomatoes with liquid, rice, water, seasoning blend, bay leaf, thyme, and hot-pepper sauce. Secure the lid. Cook on high pressure for 15 minutes. Quickly release the pressure. Remove the pressure cooker lid.

3. Set on sauté. Heat until simmering. Add the shrimp. Cook for 5 minutes, or until the shrimp are pink on the outside, stirring frequently. Turn off the pressure cooker. Let stand for 5 minutes. Discard the bay leaf. Sprinkle the jambalaya with the parsley.

SERVES 4; 1¼ cups per serving

PER SERVING Calories 255 / Total Fat 3.5 g Saturated Fat 0.5 g Trans Fat 0.0 g Polyunsaturated Fat 0.5 g
Monounsaturated Fat 2.0 g / Cholesterol 183 mg / Sodium 181 mg / Carbohydrates 29 g / Fiber 4 g /
Sugars 7 g / Protein 27 g / Dietary Exchanges 1 starch, 3 vegetable, 3 lean meat

EASY INSTANT CIOPPINO

Fisherman's Wharf in San Francisco is the home of this Italian seafood stew. In the late 1800s, fishermen often made a stew while out on their boats, and soon stands and restaurants along the wharf started ladling up a version. This tomato-based stew contained the leftover seafood from the day's catch and was flavored with onions, garlic, and herbs. Cioppino's popularity grew until it became a local favorite. Now, with this easy version, anyone can enjoy a bowl.

Total prep, cooking, and pressure release time: 35 minutes

2 teaspoons olive oil

1 small onion, chopped

1 medium rib of celery, leaves discarded, chopped

3 medium garlic cloves, minced

2 14.5-ounce cans no-salt-added diced tomatoes, undrained

1 cup fat-free, low-sodium chicken broth or Chicken Stock, such as on page 39

1 teaspoon dried oregano, crumbled

½ teaspoon pepper (coarsely ground preferred)

1 medium dried bay leaf

¼ teaspoon salt

¼ teaspoon crushed red pepper flakes

8 ounces cod fillets, rinsed and patted dry, cut into 2-inch pieces

4 fresh debearded and rinsed small mussels

8 ounces raw medium shrimp, peeled and deveined, rinsed, and patted dry

1. Heat the oil in the pressure cooker on sauté. Cook the onion and celery for 3 minutes, or until soft, stirring frequently. Add the garlic. Cook for 30 seconds, stirring frequently. Turn off the pressure cooker.

2. Stir in the tomatoes with liquid, broth, oregano, pepper, bay leaf, salt, and red pepper flakes. Secure the lid. Cook on high pressure for 10 minutes. Quickly release the pressure. Remove the pressure cooker lid.

3. Discard the bay leaf. Set the pressure cooker to sauté. Stir the fish, mussels, and shrimp into the stew. Cook for 2 to 3 minutes, or until the fish flakes easily when tested with a fork, the mussels open, and the shrimp turn pink on the outside, stirring occasionally. Don't overcook the seafood. Discard any mussels that don't open.

SERVES 4; 1½ cups per serving

PER SERVING Calories 191 / Total Fat 3.5 g Saturated Fat 0.5 g Trans Fat 0.0 g Polyunsaturated Fat 0.5 g Monounsaturated Fat 2.0 g / Cholesterol 117 mg / Sodium 338 mg / Carbohydrates 14 g / Fiber 3 g / Sugars 8 g / Protein 25 g / Dietary Exchanges 3 vegetable, 3 lean meat

Poultry

SAFFRON CHICKEN
with Brown Rice

The saffron adds a unique flavor and golden color to this updated version of chicken and rice.

Total prep, cooking, and pressure release time: 29 minutes

2 teaspoons olive oil

4 boneless, skinless chicken breast halves (about 4 ounces each), all visible fat discarded

½ cup chopped shallots

1 medium rib of celery, leaves discarded, sliced

2 medium garlic cloves, minced

¼ teaspoon saffron threads or ground turmeric

1 14.5-ounce can no-salt-added diced tomatoes, undrained

2 cups cooked brown rice

2 tablespoons minced Italian (flat-leaf) parsley

1. Heat the oil in the pressure cooker on sauté. Cook the chicken for 4 to 6 minutes, turning to brown all over. Remove the chicken from the cooker.

2. Put the shallots and celery in the pressure cooker. Cook for 3 minutes, stirring frequently. Add the garlic and saffron. Cook for 30 seconds, stirring frequently. Stir in the tomatoes with liquid. Place the chicken on the tomato mixture. Secure the lid. Cook on high pressure for 6 minutes. Allow the pressure to release naturally for 5 minutes, then quickly release any remaining pressure.

3. Spoon the rice onto plates. Serve the chicken on the rice. Spoon the sauce over the chicken. Sprinkle with the parsley.

COOK'S TIP ON PREPARING BROWN RICE: Remember to omit the salt and margarine when you're cooking the brown rice for this (or any) recipe.

SERVES 4; 3 ounces chicken and ½ cup rice per serving

PER SERVING Calories 300 / Total Fat 6.0 g Saturated Fat 1.0 g Trans Fat 0.0 g Polyunsaturated Fat 1.0 g Monounsaturated Fat 3.0 g / Cholesterol 73 mg / Sodium 160 mg / Carbohydrates 31 g / Fiber 3 g / Sugars 5 g / Protein 28 g / Dietary Exchanges 1½ starch, 2 vegetable, 3 lean meat

HERBED CHICKEN and ROOT VEGETABLES

The root vegetables absorb flavors from a citrus duo—orange and lemon—to brighten up this dish. You can alter the vegetables and herbs to match your family's preferences. Try sweet potatoes for the red potatoes. Substitute basil and thyme or tarragon for the sage and rosemary.

Total prep, cooking, and pressure release time: 31 minutes

1 teaspoon canola or corn oil

4 boneless, skinless chicken breast halves (about 4 ounces each), all visible fat discarded

4 small unpeeled red potatoes (about 1½ inches in diameter), halved

4 medium carrots, halved lengthwise

2 medium parsnips, peeled and halved lengthwise

1 medium onion, cut into 8 wedges

½ teaspoon pepper (coarsely ground preferred)

½ teaspoon dried rubbed sage

½ teaspoon dried rosemary, crushed

½ cup fat-free, low-sodium chicken broth or Chicken Stock, such as on page 39

1 tablespoon all-fruit orange marmalade

1 tablespoon fresh lemon juice

1. Heat the oil in the pressure cooker on sauté. Cook the chicken for 4 to 6 minutes, turning to brown all over. Turn off the pressure cooker.

2. Arrange the potatoes, carrots, parsnips, and onion on the chicken. Sprinkle the pepper, sage, and rosemary over all. Pour the broth around the chicken and vegetables. Secure the lid. Cook on high pressure for 6 minutes. Allow the pressure to release naturally for 5 minutes, then quickly release any remaining pressure.

3. In a small bowl, whisk together the marmalade and lemon juice. Remove the pressure cooker lid. Brush the mixture over the chicken and vegetables. Re-cover the pressure cooker. Let stand for 1 minute.

4. Remove the pressure cooker lid. Transfer the chicken and vegetables to a platter.

SERVES 4; 3 ounces chicken and ⅔ cup vegetables per serving

PER SERVING Calories 277 / Total Fat 4.5 g Saturated Fat 1.0 g Trans Fat 0.0 g Polyunsaturated Fat 1.0 g Monounsaturated Fat 1.5 g / Cholesterol 73 mg / Sodium 206 mg / Carbohydrates 32 g / Fiber 7 g / Sugars 11 g / Protein 27 g / Dietary Exchanges 1½ starch, 2 vegetable, 3 lean meat

CHEESY CHICKEN ARTICHOKE RISOTTO

Say goodbye to the constant stirring that stovetop risotto usually requires and say hello to all the creamy goodness in this one-pot meal!

Total prep, cooking, and pressure release time: 23 minutes

2 teaspoons olive oil

4 boneless, skinless chicken breast halves (about 4 ounces each), all visible fat discarded, flattened to ¼-inch thickness

2 medium shallots, chopped

2 medium garlic cloves, minced

1 cup uncooked Arborio rice

8 ounces frozen artichoke hearts

2 cups fat-free, low-sodium chicken broth or Chicken Stock, such as on page 39

1 cup frozen green peas, thawed

¼ cup shredded or grated Parmesan cheese

2 tablespoons minced fresh Italian (flat-leaf) parsley

1. Heat the oil in the pressure cooker on sauté. Cook the chicken for 4 to 6 minutes, turning to brown all over. Remove the chicken from the cooker.

2. Put the shallots in the pressure cooker. Cook for 2 to 3 minutes, or until soft, stirring frequently. Add the garlic. Cook for 30 seconds, stirring frequently. Add the rice. Cook until the rice begins to brown and is translucent, stirring frequently. Stir in the artichokes. Pour the broth over the rice mixture. Scrape the sides of the pressure cooker to keep all the food in the liquid. Place the chicken in the rice mixture. Secure the lid. Cook on high pressure for 5 minutes. Quickly release the pressure.

3. Transfer the chicken to a plate. Stir the peas and Parmesan into the rice mixture. Transfer the rice to a platter. Place the chicken on the rice. Sprinkle with the parsley.

SERVES 4; 1 cup per serving

PER SERVING Calories 396 / Total Fat 6.5 g Saturated Fat 2.0 g Trans Fat 0.0 g Polyunsaturated Fat 1.0 g Monounsaturated Fat 3.0 g / Cholesterol 76 mg / Sodium 315 mg / Carbohydrates 48 g / Fiber 7 g / Sugars 2 g / Protein 33 g / Dietary Exchanges 3 starch, 1 vegetable, 3 lean meat

CHICKEN with Apricots and Sweet Potatoes

The distinctive sweetness of apricots and the hint of orange shine in this recipe. Serve this dish with a dark green, leafy salad for an appealing color contrast on the plate.

Total prep, cooking, and pressure release time: 29 minutes

2 teaspoons canola or corn oil

4 boneless, skinless chicken breast halves (about 4 ounces each), all visible fat discarded

2 medium sweet potatoes, peeled, halved lengthwise, and cut into 2-inch pieces

½ cup dried apricot halves (about 12)

2 tablespoons grated orange zest

¼ cup fresh orange juice

½ teaspoon pepper (coarsely ground preferred)

¼ teaspoon salt

¼ cup plus 2 tablespoons fat-free, low-sodium chicken broth, or Chicken Stock, such as on page 39

1. Heat the oil in the pressure cooker on sauté. Cook the chicken for 4 to 6 minutes, turning to brown all over. Turn off the pressure cooker.

2. Arrange the sweet potatoes around the chicken. Top with the apricots, orange zest, orange juice, pepper, and salt. Pour the broth over all. Secure the lid. Cook on high pressure for 6 minutes. Allow the pressure to release naturally for 5 minutes, then quickly release any remaining pressure. Remove the pressure cooker lid.

3. Using a slotted spoon, transfer the chicken and sweet potatoes to a platter (leave the apricots in the cooker). Cover to keep warm.

4. Set the pressure cooker to sauté. Heat the sauce until simmering. Cook for 3 minutes, or until the sauce has reduced slightly and the apricots are tender, stirring frequently. Spoon the apricots and sauce over the chicken and sweet potatoes.

SERVES 4; 3 ounces chicken and 3 tablespoons sauce per serving

PER SERVING Calories 271 / Total Fat 5.5 g Saturated Fat 1.0 g Trans Fat 0.0 g Polyunsaturated Fat 1.0 g Monounsaturated Fat 2.5 g / Cholesterol 73 mg / Sodium 331 mg / Carbohydrates 29 g / Fiber 4 g / Sugars 14 g / Protein 26 g / Dietary Exchanges 1 starch, 1 fruit, 3 lean meat

HURRY-UP FROZEN CHICKEN CURRY

Did you forget to take something out of the freezer for dinner tonight? No worries. This meal comes together from freezer to table in just about 45 minutes. No thawing necessary!

Total prep, cooking, and pressure release time: 47 minutes

2 teaspoons canola or corn oil

1 medium onion, chopped

2 tablespoons minced peeled gingerroot

2 medium garlic cloves, minced

4 frozen boneless, skinless chicken breast halves (about 4 ounces each), all visible fat discarded (see Cook's Tip on page 83)

2 medium potatoes, quartered

2 medium carrots, cut into 1-inch pieces

2 tablespoons curry powder

½ teaspoon pepper (coarsely ground preferred)

¼ teaspoon salt

1 cup fat-free, low-sodium chicken broth or Chicken Stock, such as on page 39

1 tablespoon cornstarch

2 tablespoons cold water

1. Heat the oil in the pressure cooker on sauté. Cook the onion for 3 minutes, or until soft, stirring frequently. Add the gingerroot and garlic. Cook for 30 seconds, stirring frequently. Turn off the pressure cooker.

2. Push the onion to the sides of the pressure cooker. Arrange the frozen chicken breasts in a single layer on the bottom of the cooker. Spoon the onion over the chicken. Add the potatoes and carrots. Sprinkle the curry powder, pepper, and salt over all. Pour the broth over all. Secure the lid. Cook on high pressure for 15 minutes. Allow the pressure to release naturally for 10 minutes, then quickly release any remaining pressure. Remove the pressure cooker lid.

3. Transfer the chicken, potatoes, and carrots to a deep platter. Cover to keep warm.

4. Set the pressure cooker to sauté. Heat the sauce until simmering. Put the cornstarch in a small bowl. Add the water, whisking to dissolve. Whisk the cornstarch mixture into the sauce. Cook for about 1 minute, or until the sauce thickens, whisking constantly. Spoon the sauce over the chicken and vegetables.

COOK'S TIP: For the best results and even cooking, freeze the chicken in anticipation of preparing this recipe. Discard any visible fat, then arrange the chicken breasts in a single layer on a tray or baking sheet lined with cooking parchment. Freeze for about 2 hours, or until firm. Transfer to a resealable freezer bag, separating the chicken breasts with pieces of parchment.

COOK'S TIP: If you enjoy spicier food, increase the curry powder by 1 to 2 teaspoons.

SERVES 4; 3 ounces chicken and 1 cup sauce per serving

PER SERVING Calories 256 / Total Fat 6.0 g Saturated Fat 1.0 g Trans Fat 0.0 g Polyunsaturated Fat 1.0 g Monounsaturated Fat 2.5 g / Cholesterol 73 mg / Sodium 321 mg / Carbohydrates 24 g / Fiber 4 g / Sugars 5 g / Protein 27 g / Dietary Exchanges 1 starch, 2 vegetable, 3 lean meat

CHICKEN SHAWARMA

Chicken *shawarma* is a garlicky Middle Eastern dish. While it's often served in a pita, it's equally delicious served on a bed of romaine and topped with cucumbers, tomatoes, and feta. This easy-to-make dish will become a favorite go-to on those extra-busy nights.

Total prep, cooking, and pressure release time: 25 minutes

2 teaspoons olive oil

1 small onion, chopped

1 pound boneless, skinless chicken breasts, all visible fat discarded, cut into ½ x 2-inch strips

½ cup fat-free, low-sodium chicken broth or Chicken Stock, such as on page 39

4 medium garlic cloves, minced

1 teaspoon ground cumin

1 teaspoon paprika

½ teaspoon ground turmeric

½ teaspoon pepper (coarsely ground preferred)

¼ teaspoon salt

½ medium unpeeled cucumber, sliced, and ½ medium unpeeled cucumber, chopped, divided use

1 medium tomato, sliced, and 1 medium tomato, chopped, divided use

2 cups torn romaine

2 tablespoons minced fresh Italian (flat-leaf) parsley

2 tablespoons crumbled low-fat feta cheese

1. Heat the oil in the pressure cooker on sauté. Cook the onion for 3 minutes, or until soft, stirring frequently. Add the chicken. Cook the chicken for 4 to 6 minutes, or until lightly browned, stirring frequently. Turn off the pressure cooker.

2. Stir in the broth, garlic, cumin, paprika, turmeric, pepper, and salt. Secure the lid. Cook on high pressure for 4 minutes. Quickly release the pressure.

3. Arrange as follows on a platter: the sliced cucumber, sliced tomato, and romaine. Using a slotted spoon, place the chicken on the romaine. Top with the remaining chopped cucumber and chopped tomato. Sprinkle with the parsley and feta.

SERVES 4; 3 ounces chicken, ¾ cup vegetables, and 1½ teaspoons feta per serving

PER SERVING Calories 202 / Total Fat 6.0 g Saturated Fat 1.5 g Trans Fat 0.0 g Polyunsaturated Fat 1.0 g Monounsaturated Fat 2.5 g / Cholesterol 74 mg / Sodium 356 mg / Carbohydrates 9 g / Fiber 3 g / Sugars 5 g / Protein 27 g / Dietary Exchanges 2 vegetable, 3 lean meat

HARISSA CHICKEN STEW

This stew gets a flavor boost from harissa paste, a spicy condiment. The yogurt soothes the "medium" heat and the result is a comforting, delicious dish.

Total prep, cooking, and pressure release time: 38 minutes

2 teaspoons olive oil

1 small red onion, chopped

½ medium red bell pepper, chopped

1 pound boneless, skinless chicken breasts, all visible fat discarded, cut into ¾-inch pieces

3 medium garlic cloves, minced

1 15.5-ounce can no-salt-added Great Northern beans, rinsed and drained

1 14.5-ounce can no-salt-added diced tomatoes, undrained

3 medium carrots, thinly sliced

2½ tablespoons harissa paste and ½ teaspoon harissa paste, divided use

2 tablespoons water

½ teaspoon ground cumin

½ cup fat-free plain Greek yogurt

1 teaspoon fresh lemon juice

1. Heat the oil in the pressure cooker on sauté. Cook the onion for 3 minutes, or until soft, stirring frequently. Add the bell pepper. Cook for 2 minutes, stirring frequently. Add the chicken. Cook for 3 minutes, stirring frequently. Add the garlic. Cook for 30 seconds, stirring frequently. Turn off the pressure cooker.

2. Add the beans, tomatoes with liquid, carrots, 2½ tablespoons harissa paste, the water, and cumin. Secure the lid. Cook on high pressure for 5 minutes. Allow the pressure to release naturally for 10 minutes, then quickly release any remaining pressure.

3. In a small bowl, whisk together the yogurt, lemon juice, and the remaining ½ teaspoon harissa paste. Dollop each serving with the yogurt mixture.

COOK'S TIP ON HARISSA PASTE: This condiment comes from Tunisia in North Africa and is a spicy-hot blend of chiles, olive oil, garlic, and spices, such as coriander, cumin, and caraway. The spicy paste can be added to any soup or stew for a flavor punch. The degree of heat may vary with the brand. If you prefer milder flavors, add about half the amount listed in the recipe the first time you make a dish.

SERVES 4; 1½ cups per serving

PER SERVING Calories 316 / Total Fat 6.5 g Saturated Fat 1.0 g Trans Fat 0.0 g Polyunsaturated Fat 1.0 g Monounsaturated Fat 2.5 g / Cholesterol 73 mg / Sodium 451 mg / Carbohydrates 31 g / Fiber 10 g / Sugars 9 g / Protein 33 g / Dietary Exchanges 1 starch, 3 vegetable, 3½ lean meat

CHICKEN PAPRIKA with Chickpeas

This hearty dish uses familiar ingredients that are probably already in your pantry. The smoked paprika transforms the chickpeas, chicken, and potatoes into a richly flavored stew.

Total prep, cooking, and pressure release time: 1 hour 43 minutes

2 cups water

½ cup dried chickpeas, sorted for stones and shriveled peas, rinsed, and drained

2 teaspoons canola or corn oil

1 medium onion, cut into 8 wedges

1 pound boneless, skinless chicken breasts, all visible fat discarded, cut into 1-inch pieces

2 medium garlic cloves, minced

2 medium potatoes, cubed

1 cup fat-free, low-sodium chicken broth or Chicken Stock, such as on page 39

1 tablespoon paprika (smoked preferred)

¼ teaspoon pepper (coarsely ground preferred)

1 tablespoon cornstarch

1 tablespoon cold water

1. Put the water and chickpeas in the pressure cooker. Secure the lid. Cook on high pressure for 40 minutes. Allow the pressure to release naturally. Drain well in a colander.

2. Heat the oil in the pressure cooker on sauté. Cook the onion for 3 minutes, or until soft, stirring frequently. Add the chicken. Cook for 3 minutes, stirring frequently. Add the garlic. Cook for 30 seconds, stirring frequently. Turn off the pressure cooker.

3. Add the potatoes, broth, paprika, and pepper. Stir in the chickpeas. Secure the lid. Cook on high pressure for 6 minutes. Allow the pressure to release naturally for 5 minutes, then quickly release any remaining pressure. Remove the pressure cooker lid.

4. Set the pressure cooker to sauté. Heat the stew until simmering. Put the cornstarch in a small bowl. Add the cold water, whisking to dissolve. Stir the cornstarch mixture into the stew. Cook for about 1 minute, or until the stew thickens, stirring constantly.

SERVES 4; 1¼ cups per serving

PER SERVING Calories 314 / Total Fat 7.0 g Saturated Fat 1.0 g Trans Fat 0.0 g Polyunsaturated Fat 1.5 g Monounsaturated Fat 3.0 g / Cholesterol 73 mg / Sodium 155 mg / Carbohydrates 33 g / Fiber 6 g / Sugars 5 g / Protein 31 g / Dietary Exchanges 2 starch, 3½ lean meat

SPICY CHICKEN
on Shredded Lettuce

The lettuce takes the place of the ordinary bed of rice in this Asian-inspired recipe—and adds the perfect crunch.

Total prep, cooking, and pressure release time: 30 minutes

2 teaspoons canola or corn oil

4 boneless, skinless chicken breast halves (about 4 ounces each), all visible fat discarded, cut into bite-size pieces

⅔ cup finely diced celery

⅔ cup shredded carrot

⅔ cup diced onion

½ cup fat-free, low-sodium chicken broth or Chicken Stock, such as on page 39

2 tablespoons soy sauce (lowest sodium available)

1 tablespoon grated peeled gingerroot

½ teaspoon crushed red pepper flakes

2 tablespoons cornstarch

¼ cup cold water

4 cups shredded Boston or butter lettuce or romaine

Fresh parsley, for garnish

1. Heat the oil in the pressure cooker on sauté. Cook the chicken for 4 to 6 minutes, stirring to brown all over.

2. Stir in the celery, carrot, onion, broth, soy sauce, gingerroot, and red pepper flakes. Secure the lid. Cook on high pressure for 6 minutes. Allow the pressure to release naturally for about 5 minutes, then quickly release any remaining pressure. Remove the pressure cooker lid.

3. Set the pressure cooker to sauté. Heat the chicken mixture until simmering. Put the cornstarch in a small bowl. Add the water, whisking to dissolve. Stir the cornstarch mixture into the chicken mixture. Heat for about 1 minute, or until thickened, stirring constantly. Turn off the pressure cooker.

4. Put the lettuce on plates. Spoon the chicken mixture over the lettuce. Top with parsley and serve.

SERVES 4; 1 cup chicken mixture and 1 cup lettuce per serving

PER SERVING Calories 201 / Total Fat 5.5 g Saturated Fat 1.0 g Trans Fat 0.0 g Polyunsaturated Fat 1.0 g Monounsaturated Fat 2.5 g / Cholesterol 73 mg / Sodium 360 mg / Carbohydrates 11 g / Fiber 2 g / Sugars 4 g / Protein 26 g / Dietary Exchanges 2 vegetable, 3 lean meat

SALSA CHICKEN TACOS

Tacos in the pressure cooker? Enjoy flavors from across the border any night of the week. Serve with Mexican Street Corn with Quinoa (page 145).

Total prep, cooking, and pressure release time: 34 minutes

2 teaspoons canola or corn oil

1 small onion, chopped

2 teaspoons chili powder

1 teaspoon ground cumin

¼ teaspoon pepper (coarsely ground preferred)

4 boneless, skinless chicken breast halves (about 4 ounces each), all visible fat discarded

⅔ cup salsa (lowest sodium available)

2 tablespoons fresh lime juice

8 6-inch corn tortillas, warmed

2 cups shredded lettuce, such as romaine

1 small tomato, diced

2 medium green onions, chopped

3 tablespoons minced fresh cilantro

1. Heat the oil in the pressure cooker on sauté. Cook the onion for 3 minutes, or until soft, stirring frequently. Turn off the pressure cooker.

2. In a small bowl, stir together the chili powder, cumin, and pepper. Put the chicken in the pressure cooker. Sprinkle the chili powder mixture over the chicken. Using your fingertips, gently press the mixture so it adheres to the chicken. Pour the salsa and lime juice over the chicken. Secure the lid. Cook on high pressure for 6 minutes. Allow the pressure to release naturally for 5 minutes, then quickly release any remaining pressure.

3. Transfer the chicken to a plate. Let stand for 5 minutes. Cut the chicken into strips or using the tines of a fork, shred the chicken.

4. Place the chicken in the center of the tortillas. Top with the lettuce, tomato, and green onions. Sprinkle with the cilantro. Fold the sides of the tortillas together. You can use a long, wooden pick to hold together for serving if desired.

SERVES 4; 2 tacos per serving

PER SERVING Calories 254 / **Total Fat** 6.5 g Saturated Fat 1.0 g Trans Fat 0.0 g Polyunsaturated Fat 1.5 g Monounsaturated Fat 2.5 g / **Cholesterol** 73 mg / **Sodium** 361 mg / **Carbohydrates** 22 g / **Fiber** 3 g / Sugars 4 g / **Protein** 27 g / **Dietary Exchanges** 1 starch, 1 vegetable, 3 lean meat

CHICKEN GYROS with Tzatziki Sauce

Transport yourself to Greece with this meal. Enjoy with Creamy Hummus (page 32).

Total prep, cooking, and pressure release time: 32 minutes

2 teaspoons olive oil

1 medium onion, thinly sliced

2 medium garlic cloves, minced

6 boneless, skinless chicken breast halves (about 4 ounces each), all visible fat discarded

1 teaspoon ground cumin

1 teaspoon dried oregano, crumbled

½ teaspoon salt-free lemon pepper

2 tablespoons fresh lemon juice

½ cup fat-free, low-sodium chicken broth or Chicken Stock, such as on page 39

SAUCE

½ cup finely chopped peeled cucumber

½ cup fat-free plain Greek yogurt

2 teaspoons fresh lemon juice

1 medium garlic clove, minced

½ teaspoon dried dillweed, crumbled

6 6-inch whole-grain pitas (lowest sodium available)

1½ cups chopped romaine

1 cup chopped tomatoes

1. Heat the oil in the pressure cooker on sauté. Cook the onion for 3 minutes, or until soft, stirring frequently. Add the garlic. Cook for 30 seconds, stirring frequently. Turn off the pressure cooker.

2. Put the chicken in the pressure cooker. In a small bowl, stir together the cumin, oregano, and lemon pepper. Sprinkle the mixture over the chicken. Using your fingertips, gently press the mixture so it adheres to the chicken. Drizzle the lemon juice over all. Pour the broth around the chicken. Secure the lid. Cook on high pressure for 6 minutes. Allow the pressure to release naturally for 5 minutes, then quickly release any remaining pressure.

3. Transfer the chicken to a plate. Let stand for 5 minutes. Cut the chicken into strips or using the tines of a fork, shred the chicken.

4. In a small bowl, stir together the sauce ingredients. Top the pitas with the chicken, romaine, tomatoes, and sauce.

SERVES 6; 1 gyro per serving

PER SERVING Calories 336 / Total Fat 6.5 g Saturated Fat 1.0 g Trans Fat 0.0 g Polyunsaturated Fat 1.5 g Monounsaturated Fat 2.0 g / Cholesterol 74 mg / Sodium 467 mg / Carbohydrates 39 g / Fiber 6 g / Sugars 4 g / Protein 33 g / Dietary Exchanges 2 starch, 1 vegetable, 3 lean meat

Chicken Gyros with Tzatziki
Sauce, page 91

TURKEY
with Sage and Sweet Potatoes

Turkey and sweet potatoes are a popular combination for holiday meals, but why wait for the holidays? In this recipe, these two complementary ingredients combine to make an easy dinner—one that cooks so quickly you can even enjoy it on the busiest evening.

Total prep, cooking, and pressure release time: 20 minutes

3 medium garlic cloves, minced

2 teaspoons dried rubbed sage

½ teaspoon dried thyme, crumbled

½ teaspoon pepper (coarsely ground preferred)

¼ teaspoon salt

1 1-pound turkey tenderloin, all visible fat discarded, cut into 2-inch pieces

1 cup fat-free, low-sodium chicken broth or Chicken Stock, such as on page 39

2 medium sweet potatoes (about 8 ounces each), peeled and quartered

1. In a small bowl, stir together the garlic, sage, thyme, pepper, and salt. Sprinkle half the mixture over the turkey. Using your fingertips, gently press the mixture so it adheres to the turkey. Place the turkey in the pressure cooker. Pour the broth around the turkey.

2. Place the steaming rack over the turkey. Place the sweet potatoes on the rack. Sprinkle the remaining seasoning mixture over the sweet potatoes. Secure the lid. Cook on high pressure for 7 minutes. Quickly release the pressure.

3. Serve the sweet potatoes with the turkey.

SERVES 4; 3 ounces turkey and ½ sweet potato per serving

PER SERVING Calories 232 / Total Fat 1.0 g Saturated Fat 0.5 g Trans Fat 0.0 g Polyunsaturated Fat 0.5 g Monounsaturated Fat 0.0 g / Cholesterol 77 mg / Sodium 273 mg / Carbohydrates 24 g / Fiber 4 g / Sugars 5 g / Protein 30 g / Dietary Exchanges 1½ starch, 3 lean meat

THAI-SPICED TURKEY SLIDERS
with Cilantro Slaw

These mini sandwiches are the ideal fun dinner to serve when family and friends gather at your house to watch sports. The turkey is a bit spicy, but it contrasts perfectly with the cooling slaw.

Total prep, cooking, and pressure release time: 21 minutes

2 teaspoons canola or corn oil

1 pound ground skinless turkey or chicken breast

1 cup fat-free, low-sodium chicken broth or Chicken Stock, such as on page 39

1 Thai or serrano pepper, halved, seeds and ribs discarded, minced

2 tablespoons minced fresh cilantro

2 tablespoons minced peeled gingerroot

2 tablespoons fresh lime juice and 1 tablespoon fresh lime juice, divided use

1 tablespoon soy sauce (lowest sodium available)

2 medium garlic cloves, minced

1½ cups finely shredded green cabbage

2 tablespoons minced fresh cilantro

⅛ teaspoon salt

8 whole-grain slider buns (lowest sodium available), split and toasted

1. Heat the oil in the pressure cooker on sauté. Cook the turkey for 3 minutes, or until lightly browned, stirring frequently to turn and break up the turkey. Turn off the pressure cooker.

2. Stir in the broth, Thai pepper, cilantro, gingerroot, 2 tablespoons lime juice, the soy sauce, and garlic. Secure the lid. Cook on high pressure for 3 minutes. Quickly release the pressure.

3. Meanwhile, in a medium bowl, stir together the cabbage, cilantro, salt, and the remaining 1 tablespoon lime juice.

4. Divide the turkey among the slider buns. Top with the slaw.

SERVES 4; 2 sliders per serving

PER SERVING Calories 352 / Total Fat 7.0 g Saturated Fat 1.0 g Trans Fat 0.0 g Polyunsaturated Fat 2.5 g Monounsaturated Fat 2.5 g / Cholesterol 77 mg / Sodium 570 mg / Carbohydrates 40 g / Fiber 6 g / Sugars 8 g / Protein 35 g / Dietary Exchanges 2½ starch, 3 lean meat

MANGO-GLAZED TURKEY MEATBALLS

The mango glaze, accented with ginger, garlic, balsamic vinegar, honey, and red pepper flakes, adds a fresh, tropical flavor to these traditional meatballs. Enjoy with Beet Salad with Citrus Vinaigrette (page 148).

Total prep, cooking, and pressure release time: 1 hour 3 minutes

⅓ cup panko (Japanese-style bread crumbs)

1 large egg white

½ teaspoon ground ginger

¼ teaspoon garlic powder

¼ teaspoon pepper (coarsely ground preferred)

1 pound ground skinless turkey breast

1 medium mango, peeled, pitted, and diced

2 tablespoons balsamic vinegar

1 tablespoon honey

1 teaspoon soy sauce (lowest sodium available)

¼ teaspoon crushed red pepper flakes

1 tablespoon canola or corn oil and 1 teaspoon canola or corn oil, divided use

¾ cup water

1. In a large bowl, stir together the panko, egg white, ginger, garlic powder, and pepper. Add the turkey, stirring until well blended. Cover and refrigerate for about 30 minutes, or until well chilled.

2. In a small bowl, stir together the mango, vinegar, honey, soy sauce, and red pepper flakes. Set aside.

3. Shape the turkey mixture into 24 meatballs, each 1 to 1¼ inches in diameter. Heat 1 tablespoon oil in the pressure cooker on sauté. Arrange about half the meatballs in a single layer in the cooker. Cook for 4 to 6 minutes, or until browned, turning to cook on all sides. Transfer the meatballs to a large plate. Repeat with the remaining 1 teaspoon oil and meatballs. Turn off the pressure cooker.

4. Return all the meatballs to the cooker. Pour the mango mixture and water over the meatballs. Secure the lid. Cook on high pressure for 3 minutes. Allow the pressure to release naturally for 5 minutes, then quickly release any remaining pressure.

5. Using a slotted spoon, transfer the meatballs to a serving bowl. Cover to keep warm.

6. Allow the sauce to cool slightly. Pour it into a blender (vent the blender lid). Puree until smooth. Pour the sauce over the meatballs. Use caution as the sauce and steam are hot. Vent the blender lid away from you.

7. Pour the sauce over the meatballs.

SERVES 4; 6 meatballs and ¼ cup sauce per serving

PER SERVING Calories 271 / **Total Fat** 6.0 g **Saturated Fat** 1.0 g **Trans Fat** 0.0 g **Polyunsaturated Fat** 1.5 g **Monounsaturated Fat** 3.5 g / **Cholesterol** 77 mg / **Sodium** 112 mg / **Carbohydrates** 24 g / **Fiber** 2 g / **Sugars** 18 g / **Protein** 30 g / **Dietary Exchanges** 1 fruit, ½ starch, 3 lean meat

Meats

BELGIAN-STYLE BEEF STEW

The unexpected ingredient in this stew is the beer; it adds a rich, earthy flavor to the stew that makes it taste as if it's been simmering for hours. Enjoy with crusty whole-grain bread and a dark green, leafy salad.

Total prep, cooking, and pressure release time: 1 hour 14 minutes

2 teaspoons canola or corn oil

1 pound boneless top round steak, all visible fat discarded, cut into 1½-inch cubes

1 medium onion, chopped

3 medium carrots, cut into thick slices

2 medium potatoes, cut into eighths

4 ounces button mushrooms, cut into thick slices

½ cup beer (regular or nonalcoholic) or water

½ cup fat-free, low-sodium beef broth or Beef Stock, such as on page 40

2 medium garlic cloves, minced

½ teaspoon dried thyme, crumbled

2 tablespoons all-purpose flour

2 tablespoons cold water

1. Heat the oil in the pressure cooker on sauté. Cook the beef, turning to brown on all sides. Using a slotted spoon, transfer the beef to a large plate.

2. Add the onion. Cook for 3 minutes, or until soft, stirring frequently. Turn off the pressure cooker.

3. Stir in the carrots, potatoes, mushrooms, beer, broth, garlic, thyme, and reserved beef. Secure the lid. Cook on high pressure for 25 minutes. Allow the pressure to release naturally. Remove the pressure cooker lid.

4. Set the pressure cooker to sauté. Heat the stew until simmering. Put the flour in a small bowl. Add the water, whisking to dissolve. Stir the flour mixture into the stew until well blended. Cook until the stew thickens, stirring constantly. Simmer for 1 minute.

COOK'S TIP: Browning the meat adds a layer of flavor, but if time is short, you can omit this step.

SERVES 4; 1½ cups per serving

PER SERVING Calories 268 / Total Fat 6.0 g Saturated Fat 1.5 g Trans Fat 0.0 g Polyunsaturated Fat 1.0 g Monounsaturated Fat 2.5 g / Cholesterol 57 mg / Sodium 84 mg / Carbohydrates 26 g / Fiber 4 g / Sugars 6 g / Protein 27 g / Dietary Exchanges 1 starch, 2 vegetable, 3 lean meat

CHICAGO BEEF SANDWICHES

This sandwich is a healthier yet satisfying version of the Chicago classic that you won't have to travel far for. You can easily make this Windy City favorite in your own kitchen.

Total prep, cooking, and pressure release time: 1 hour 25 minutes

Cooking spray

1 2-pound boneless chuck shoulder roast, all visible fat discarded

1 medium onion, thinly sliced

1 teaspoon dried basil, crumbled

1 teaspoon dried oregano, crumbled

½ teaspoon dried thyme, crumbled

¼ teaspoon crushed red pepper flakes

1 cup fat-free, low-sodium beef broth or Beef Stock, such as on page 40

3 tablespoons jarred, sliced pepperoncini peppers (lowest sodium available), drained and patted dry

4 whole-grain hoagie buns (about 4 ounces each) (lowest sodium available), split and toasted

1. Lightly spray the pressure cooker with cooking spray. Set on sauté. Cook the beef for 4 to 6 minutes, turning to brown on all sides. Transfer to a large plate. Turn off the pressure cooker.

2. Put the onion in the pressure cooker. Place the beef on the onion.

3. In a small bowl, stir together the basil, oregano, thyme, and red pepper flakes. Sprinkle the mixture over the beef. Using your fingertips, gently press the mixture so it adheres to the beef. Pour the broth around the beef. Arrange 1 tablespoon pepperoncini on the beef. Sprinkle the remaining pepperoncini around the beef. Secure the lid. Cook on high pressure for 50 minutes. Allow the pressure to release naturally for 15 minutes, then quickly release any remaining pressure. Transfer the beef to a large platter. Using two forks, shred the beef.

4. Put the bun halves on plates. Place the beef on the buns. Using a slotted spoon, place the pepperoncini on the beef. Serve the sandwiches open-face.

SERVES 8; 3 ounces beef and ½ bun per serving

PER SERVING Calories 250 / Total Fat 6.5 g Saturated Fat 2.0 g Trans Fat 0.0 g Polyunsaturated Fat 1.0 g Monounsaturated Fat 3.0 g / Cholesterol 74 mg / Sodium 337 mg / Carbohydrates 21 g / Fiber 3 g / Sugars 4 g / Protein 28 g / Dietary Exchanges 1½ starch, 3 lean meat

CHIPOTLE BEEF

Make this entrée a south-of-the-border meal and serve it with Mexican Street Corn with Quinoa (page 145).

Total prep, cooking, and pressure release time: 1 hour 11 minutes

2 teaspoons canola or corn oil

1 medium onion, halved and thinly sliced

1 medium fresh jalapeño, seeds and ribs discarded, chopped

2 medium garlic cloves, minced

1 1-pound flank steak, all visible fat discarded

1 chipotle pepper canned in adobo sauce, finely chopped

1½ teaspoons chili powder

1 teaspoon ground cumin

¼ teaspoon salt

1 14.5-ounce can no-salt-added diced tomatoes, undrained

1. Heat the oil in the pressure cooker on sauté. Cook the onion for 3 minutes, or until soft, stirring frequently. Add the jalapeño and garlic. Cook for 30 seconds, stirring constantly. Turn off the pressure cooker. Place the beef on the onion mixture.

2. In a small bowl, stir together the chipotle pepper, chili powder, cumin, and salt. Spread the mixture over the beef. Pour the tomatoes with liquid over all. Secure the lid. Cook on high pressure for 45 minutes. Allow the pressure to release naturally for 10 minutes, then quickly release any remaining pressure.

3. Transfer the beef to a cutting board. Let stand for at least 10 minutes. Cut across the grain into slices. Using a slotted spoon, spoon the onion mixture over the beef.

COOK'S TIP: You can serve the shredded beef on whole-grain tortillas. Look for tortillas with the lowest amount of sodium.

COOK'S TIP ON CHIPOTLE PEPPERS: Chipotle peppers are dried, smoked jalapeño peppers. They're usually canned in a spicy adobo sauce. You can freeze any unused peppers: Spread the peppers with the sauce in a thin layer on a plate lined with cooking parchment or wax paper. Freeze them, uncovered, for about 2 hours, or until just firm. Transfer the frozen peppers to a resealable freezer bag.

SERVES 4; 3 ounces beef and 1½ tablespoons sauce per serving

PER SERVING Calories 229 / Total Fat 9.5 g Saturated Fat 3.0 g Trans Fat 0.0 g Polyunsaturated Fat 1.0 g Monounsaturated Fat 4.0 g / Cholesterol 65 mg / Sodium 316 mg / Carbohydrates 10 g / Fiber 2 g / Sugars 6 g / Protein 24 g / Dietary Exchanges 2 vegetable, 3 lean meat

SPICED BRISKET with Cranberries

Plan to prepare and cook the brisket the day before you serve it. This way it'll give the beef time to release its juices so you can use them to make the sauce. Also, once the juices have cooled, you can easily skim off the fat. Refrigerate the brisket overnight, then the next day, before the meal, finish it up.

Total prep, cooking, and pressure release time: 1 hour 30 minutes

2 teaspoons olive oil

1 2-pound beef brisket, all visible fat discarded

1 teaspoon dried oregano, crumbled

½ teaspoon garlic powder

¼ teaspoon salt

¼ teaspoon pepper (coarsely ground preferred)

½ cup fat-free, low-sodium beef broth or Beef Stock, such as on page 40

1 cup barbecue sauce (lowest sodium available)

1 cup whole cranberries

⅓ cup firmly packed dark brown sugar

1. Heat the oil in the pressure cooker on sauté. Cook the brisket on both sides, or until browned. Turn off the pressure cooker. In a small bowl, stir together the oregano, garlic powder, salt, and pepper. Sprinkle the mixture over the beef. Pour the broth around the beef. Pour the barbecue sauce over the beef. Secure the lid. Cook on high pressure for 55 minutes. Allow the pressure to release naturally for 15 minutes, then quickly release any remaining pressure.

2. Transfer the beef to a glass baking dish. Cover and refrigerate. Pour the accumulated juices into a glass bowl. Cover and refrigerate.

3. Just before serving time, preheat the oven to 300°F. Remove the beef from the refrigerator. Very thinly slice the beef across the grain. Put it in the baking dish. Skim off the fat from the refrigerated juices. Pour 1 cup of the juices over the beef. Bake, tightly covered, for 45 minutes to 1 hour.

4. Meanwhile, in a small saucepan, cook 1 cup of the juices over medium-high heat. Add the cranberries and brown sugar. Cook until the cranberries pop and are soft, stirring occasionally. Drizzle the sauce over the beef.

SERVES 8; 3 ounces beef and 2 tablespoons sauce per serving

PER SERVING Calories 257 / Total Fat 6.0 g Saturated Fat 2.0 g Trans Fat 0.0 g Polyunsaturated Fat 0.5 g Monounsaturated Fat 3.0 g / Cholesterol 70 mg / Sodium 331 mg / Carbohydrates 24 g / Fiber 1 g / Sugars 22 g / Protein 24 g / Dietary Exchanges 1½ other carbohydrate, 3 lean meat

TEXAS-STYLE CHILI

You won't find beans in this Lone Star chili since many Texans prefer their "bowl of red" without beans. Chili powder, cumin, and oregano team up to provide the perfect blend of flavors. Masa harina, or cornmeal, is the "secret" thickener for chili.

Total prep, cooking, and pressure release time: 1 hour 6 minutes

2 teaspoons canola or corn oil

1 pound boneless top round steak, all visible fat discarded, cut into ½-inch cubes

1 medium onion, chopped

1 14.5-ounce can no-salt-added diced tomatoes, undrained

1 cup fat-free, low-sodium beef broth or Beef Stock, such as on page 40

3 tablespoons chili powder

1 tablespoon ground cumin

1 teaspoon dried oregano, crumbled

2 medium garlic cloves, minced

¼ teaspoon pepper (coarsely ground preferred)

¼ cup masa harina or yellow cornmeal

1 tablespoon fresh lime juice

1. Heat the oil in the pressure cooker on sauté. Cook the beef until browned on both sides. Add the onion. Cook for 3 minutes, or until soft, stirring frequently. Turn off the pressure cooker.

2. Stir in the tomatoes with liquid, broth, chili powder, cumin, oregano, garlic, and pepper. Secure the lid. Cook on high pressure for 25 minutes. Allow the pressure to release naturally for 15 minutes, then quickly release any remaining pressure. Remove the pressure cooker lid.

3. Stir in the masa harina and lime juice. Cook on sauté until thickened.

COOK'S TIP ON MASA HARINA: Masa harina ("dough flour") is the corn flour used to make corn tortillas. It has a distinctive flavor as the corn from which it's made is dried and then cooked in limewater. You can find it at most grocery stores in the ethnic foods aisle.

SERVES 4; 1¼ cups per serving

PER SERVING Calories 248 / Total Fat 6.5 g Saturated Fat 1.5 g Trans Fat 0.0 g Polyunsaturated Fat 1.5 g Monounsaturated Fat 3.0 g / Cholesterol 58 mg / Sodium 216 mg / Carbohydrates 19 g / Fiber 5 g / Sugars 6 g / Protein 29 g / Dietary Exchanges ½ starch, 2 vegetable, 3 lean meat

BEEF DAUBE PROVENÇAL

This version of a classic French stew has a rich, deep flavor after it's been pressure cooked. Traditionally, it's made the day ahead, refrigerated, and then heated and served. The additional time melds the herbs and beef for a robust taste. You can serve it immediately or make it ahead.

Total prep, cooking, and pressure release time: 1 hour 16 minutes

2 teaspoons olive oil

1½ pounds boneless chuck shoulder, all visible fat discarded, cut into 1-inch pieces

1¾ cups fat-free, low-sodium beef broth or Beef Stock, such as on page 40

10 ounces frozen pearl onions

½ cup red wine (regular or nonalcoholic)

¼ cup no-salt-added tomato paste

4 medium carrots, cut into 2-inch strips

4 medium ribs of celery, leaves discarded, cut into 1½-inch slices

4 medium garlic cloves, minced

1 teaspoon dried thyme, crumbled

½ teaspoon dried rosemary, crushed

1 medium dried bay leaf

3 tablespoons all-purpose flour

⅓ cup water

2 ounces pitted niçoise olives

1. Heat the oil in the pressure cooker on sauté. Cook half the beef for 4 to 6 minutes, or until browned all over. Transfer to a large plate. Repeat with the remaining beef. Turn off the pressure cooker.

2. Add the broth, onions, wine, tomato paste, carrots, celery, garlic, thyme, rosemary, and bay leaf. Stir together. Secure the lid. Cook on high pressure for 25 minutes. Allow the pressure to release naturally for 15 minutes, then quickly release any remaining pressure. Remove the pressure cooker lid.

3. Set the pressure cooker to sauté. Heat the stew until simmering. Put the flour in a small bowl. Add the water, whisking to dissolve. Stir the flour mixture into the stew until well blended. Cook until the stew thickens, stirring constantly. Simmer for 1 minute.

4. Turn off the pressure cooker. Stir in the olives. Discard the bay leaf before serving.

SERVES 6; 1 cup per serving

PER SERVING Calories 252 / Total Fat 8.5 g Saturated Fat 2.0 g Trans Fat 0.0 g Polyunsaturated Fat 1.0 g Monounsaturated Fat 4.0 g / Cholesterol 65 mg / Sodium 294 mg / Carbohydrates 19 g / Fiber 3 g / Sugars 6 g / Protein 24 g / Dietary Exchanges 3 vegetable, 3 lean meat

BEEF STROGANOFF

Stew meat becomes tender under pressure, making this version of stroganoff a hit.

Total prep, cooking, and pressure release time: 1 hour 18 minutes

2 teaspoons canola or corn oil

1 pound beef stew meat, all visible fat discarded, cut into 1-inch pieces

1 medium onion, chopped

8 ounces button mushrooms, cut into thick slices

1 cup fat-free, low-sodium beef broth or Beef Stock, such as on page 40

2 medium garlic cloves, minced

1 teaspoon Dijon mustard (lowest sodium available)

½ teaspoon dried thyme, crumbled

¼ teaspoon paprika

¼ teaspoon pepper (coarsely ground preferred)

6 ounces dried no-yolk noodles

3 tablespoons all-purpose flour

¼ cup cold water

¾ cup fat-free sour cream or fat-free plain yogurt

2 tablespoons minced fresh Italian (flat-leaf) parsley or dillweed

1. Heat the oil in the pressure cooker on sauté. Cook the beef for 4 minutes, or until browned on all sides, stirring occasionally. Add the onion. Cook for 3 minutes, or until soft, stirring frequently. Turn off the pressure cooker.

2. Stir in the mushrooms, broth, garlic, mustard, thyme, paprika, and pepper. Secure the lid. Cook on high pressure for 25 minutes. Allow the pressure to release naturally for 15 minutes, then quickly release any additional pressure. Remove the pressure cooker lid.

3. Meanwhile, prepare the noodles using the package directions, omitting the salt. Drain.

4. Set the pressure cooker to sauté. Heat the stroganoff until simmering. Put the flour in a small bowl. Add the water, whisking to dissolve. Stir the flour mixture into the stroganoff until well blended. Cook until thickened, stirring constantly. Simmer for 1 minute. Turn off the pressure cooker. Stir in the sour cream until blended.

5. Serve over the noodles. Sprinkle with the parsley.

SERVES 4; 1 cup per serving

PER SERVING Calories 440 / Total Fat 11.0 g Saturated Fat 3.0 g Trans Fat 0.0 g Polyunsaturated Fat 1.0 g
Monounsaturated Fat 5.0 g / Cholesterol 78 mg / Sodium 167 mg / Carbohydrates 50 g / Fiber 4 g /
Sugars 8 g / Protein 33 g / Dietary Exchanges 3 starch, 1 vegetable, 3 lean meat

PORK LOIN with Fennel and Mustard

The sweet notes from fennel and the zestiness of mustard add the flavor to this pork dish. Serve with baked or roasted sweet potato cubes and Pistachio-Cranberry Brussels Sprouts (page 142).

Total prep, cooking, and pressure release time: 46 minutes

1 teaspoon dried rosemary, crushed

½ teaspoon dried thyme, crumbled

¼ teaspoon pepper (coarsely ground preferred)

1 1-pound boneless pork loin roast, all visible fat discarded

2 teaspoons canola or corn oil

1 medium onion, cut into 6 wedges

2 medium fennel bulbs, quartered and cored

1 cup fat-free, low-sodium beef broth or Beef Stock, such as on page 40

1 tablespoon Dijon mustard (lowest sodium available)

1 teaspoon dry mustard

1. In a small bowl, stir together the rosemary, thyme, and pepper. Sprinkle over the pork. Using your fingertips, gently press the mixture so it adheres to the pork. Heat the oil in the pressure cooker on sauté. Cook the pork for 4 to 6 minutes, or until browned all over. Transfer to a large plate.

2. Put the onion in the pressure cooker. Cook for 3 minutes, or until the edges begin to turn golden, stirring frequently. Turn off the pressure cooker.

3. Place the reserved pork on the onion. Add the fennel.

4. In a small bowl, whisk together the broth, Dijon mustard, and dry mustard. Pour over the pork and vegetables. Secure the lid. Cook on high pressure for 15 minutes. Allow the pressure to release naturally for 10 minutes, then quickly release any remaining pressure.

SERVES 4; 3 ounces pork and ½ cup vegetables per serving

PER SERVING Calories 247 / Total Fat 11.0 g Saturated Fat 3.0 g Trans Fat 0.0 g Polyunsaturated Fat 1.5 g Monounsaturated Fat 5.0 g / Cholesterol 64 mg / Sodium 200 mg / Carbohydrates 13 g / Fiber 5 g / Sugars 3 g / Protein 25 g / Dietary Exchanges 3 vegetable, 3 lean meat

GINGERED PORK TENDERLOIN
with Plums

Just a little sweet and a little spicy describes this entrée. The pork is sprinkled with pepper and cayenne and the plums add a hint of sweetness.

Total prep, cooking, and pressure release time: 47 minutes

1 teaspoon canola or corn oil

½ teaspoon pepper (coarsely ground preferred)

⅛ teaspoon cayenne

1 1-pound pork tenderloin, all visible fat discarded, halved crosswise

1 medium red onion, thinly sliced

2 tablespoons minced peeled gingerroot

2 medium garlic cloves, minced

¾ cup fat-free, low-sodium chicken broth or Chicken Stock, such as on page 39

2 medium plums, pitted and thinly sliced

1. Heat the oil in the pressure cooker on sauté. Sprinkle the pepper and cayenne over the pork. Cook the pork for 4 to 6 minutes, turning to brown all over. Transfer the pork to a plate.

2. Put the onion in the pressure cooker. Cook for 3 minutes, or until soft, stirring frequently. Add the gingerroot and garlic. Cook for 30 seconds, stirring frequently. Turn off the pressure cooker. Return the pork to the cooker. Spoon the onion mixture over the pork.

3. Pour the broth over the pork. Secure the lid. Cook on high pressure for 6 minutes. Allow the pressure to release naturally for 10 minutes, then quickly release any remaining pressure. Remove the pressure cooker lid.

4. Transfer the pork to a cutting board. Cover to keep warm.

5. Set the pressure cooker to sauté. Add the plums to the liquid in the pressure cooker. Cook for 10 minutes, or until the plums are tender and the liquid has reduced slightly, stirring occasionally.

6. Cut the pork across the grain into slices. Transfer to plates. Using a slotted spoon, arrange the plums on the pork. Drizzle each serving with the cooking liquid.

SERVES 4; 3 ounces pork, ¼ cup plums, and 1 tablespoon sauce per serving

PER SERVING Calories 163 / Total Fat 4.0 g Saturated Fat 1.0 g Trans Fat 0.0 g Polyunsaturated Fat 1.0 g Monounsaturated Fat 2.0 g / Cholesterol 60 mg / Sodium 60 mg / Carbohydrates 9 g / Fiber 1 g / Sugars 7 g / Protein 22 g / Dietary Exchanges ½ fruit, 3 lean meat

GERMAN PORK and CABBAGE

The classic flavor combination of pork and cabbage comes alive in this dish, thanks to a splash of vinegar, fennel seeds, and dill weed. Serve with Cinnamon-Spice Applesauce (page 157).

Total prep, cooking, and pressure release time: 41 minutes

2 teaspoons canola or corn oil

1 medium onion, cut into 8 wedges

1 pound boneless pork loin, all visible fat discarded, cut into 1-inch cubes

½ medium green cabbage, cored and cut into 6 wedges (about 1½ to 2 inches wide)

1 teaspoon dried dillweed, crumbled

½ teaspoon fennel seeds

½ teaspoon pepper (coarsely ground preferred)

1 cup fat-free, low-sodium chicken broth or Chicken Stock, such as on page 39

1 tablespoon white wine vinegar

1. Heat the oil in the pressure cooker on sauté. Cook the onion for 3 minutes, or until the edges begin to turn golden, stirring frequently. Add the pork. Cook for 3 minutes, or until lightly browned, stirring frequently. Turn off the pressure cooker.

2. Stir in the cabbage. In a small bowl, stir together the dillweed, fennel seeds, and pepper. Sprinkle over the cabbage. Pour the broth and vinegar over all. Secure the lid. Cook on high pressure for 5 minutes. Allow the pressure to release naturally for 10 minutes, then quickly release any remaining pressure.

SERVES 4; 3 ounces pork and 2 cups vegetables per serving

PER SERVING Calories 232 / Total Fat 10.0 g Saturated Fat 3.0 g Trans Fat 0.0 g Polyunsaturated Fat 1.5 g
Monounsaturated Fat 5.0 g / Cholesterol 64 mg / Sodium 83 mg / Carbohydrates 10 g / Fiber 4 g /
Sugars 6 g / Protein 25 g / Dietary Exchanges 2 vegetable, 3 lean meat

PORK TACOS with Pineapple Salsa

Tacos al pastor, now a popular entrée at restaurants, are the inspiration for this recipe. This Central Mexico specialty features grilled meat and is flavored with pineapple. For these tacos, the pressure cooker replaces the grill. Pineapple does double duty—the juice flavors the meat, while the crushed pineapple is used in the salsa. The result is a fresh twist on tacos.

Total prep, cooking, and pressure release time: 42 minutes

1 8-ounce can crushed pineapple in its own juice, well drained, juice reserved

¼ cup finely chopped red onion

2 tablespoons minced fresh cilantro and (optional) fresh cilantro leaves for garnish, divided use

1 tablespoon fresh lime juice

½ medium fresh jalapeño, seeds and ribs discarded, chopped, and ½ medium fresh jalapeño, seeds and ribs discarded, chopped, divided use

⅛ teaspoon salt and ⅛ teaspoon salt, divided use

1 1-pound pork tenderloin, all visible fat discarded, halved crosswise

¾ cup fat-free, low-sodium chicken broth or Chicken Stock, such as on page 39

2 medium garlic cloves, minced

1 teaspoon ground cumin

1 teaspoon dried oregano, crumbled

8 6-inch corn tortillas

2 radishes, thinly sliced

1. In a small bowl, stir together the pineapple, onion, minced cilantro, lime juice, ½ jalapeño, and ⅛ teaspoon salt. Set aside.

2. Place the pork in the pressure cooker. Add the broth, garlic, cumin, and oregano. Add ¼ cup of the reserved pineapple juice and the remaining ½ jalapeño and ⅛ teaspoon salt. Secure the lid. Cook on high pressure for 7 minutes. Allow the pressure to release naturally for 10 minutes, then quickly release any remaining pressure.

3. Transfer the pork to a cutting board. Let stand, covered, for 5 minutes. Meanwhile, warm the tortillas using the package directions.

4. Finely chop the pork. Spoon the pork onto the tortillas. Top with the salsa. Garnish with the radishes and the remaining cilantro leaves.

SERVES 4; 3 ounces pork, 2 corn tortillas, and ¼ cup salsa per serving

PER SERVING Calories 226 / Total Fat 3.5 g Saturated Fat 1.0 g Trans Fat 0.0 g Polyunsaturated Fat 0.5 g Monounsaturated Fat 1.5 g / Cholesterol 60 mg / Sodium 257 mg / Carbohydrates 24 g / Fiber 2 g / Sugars 8 g / Protein 24 g / Dietary Exchanges 1 starch, ½ fruit, 3 lean meat

LAMB BIRYANI

Biryani is a one-dish meal that's very popular in India. Although there are many versions, it's basically a mixture of rice, herbs, spices, vegetables, meat, and yogurt.

Total prep, cooking, and pressure release time: 38 minutes

2 teaspoons canola or corn oil

½ cup diced onion

1 pound lamb shoulder, all visible fat discarded, cut into 1-inch cubes

½ cup fat-free plain Greek yogurt

½ cup minced fresh cilantro and chopped fresh cilantro for garnish, divided use

¼ cup chopped fresh mint

1 tablespoon minced peeled gingerroot

2 teaspoons garam masala

3 medium garlic cloves, minced

1 teaspoon ground turmeric

¼ teaspoon ground cinnamon

1 cup uncooked instant brown rice

1 cup canned no-salt-added diced tomatoes, undrained

1 cup water

½ cup golden or dark raisins

1. Heat the oil in the pressure cooker on sauté. Cook the onion for 3 minutes, or until soft, stirring frequently. Transfer to a plate. Put the lamb in the pressure cooker. Cook on sauté for 4 to 6 minutes, or until lightly browned, stirring frequently. Turn off the pressure cooker.

2. Return the onion to the pressure cooker. Stir together with the lamb. Add the yogurt, ½ cup minced cilantro, the mint, gingerroot, garam masala, garlic, turmeric, and cinnamon. Stir well. Top with the rice, spreading in a single layer. Pour the tomatoes with liquid over the rice. Pour in the water. Using a spoon, submerge the rice in the liquid. Secure the lid. Cook on high pressure for 10 minutes. Quickly release the pressure.

3. Just before serving, sprinkle with the raisins or stir them in. Garnish with the remaining chopped cilantro.

COOK'S TIP: If you prefer a spicier biryani, add ¼ to ½ teaspoon cayenne to the spices.

SERVES 4; 1 generous cup per serving

PER SERVING Calories 360 / Total Fat 10.5 g Saturated Fat 3.0 g Trans Fat 0.0 g Polyunsaturated Fat 1.5 g Monounsaturated Fat 5.0 g / Cholesterol 63 mg / Sodium 71 mg / Carbohydrates 41 g / Fiber 3 g / Sugars 16 g / Protein 25 g / Dietary Exchanges 1 starch, 2 vegetable, 1 fruit, 3 lean meat

Vegetarian Entrées

FIREHOUSE THREE-BEAN CHILI

This chili is ready in under 45 minutes, but it's packed with flavor like it was simmered all day long. Protein-rich beans make this a go-to vegetarian meal.

Total prep, cooking, and pressure release time: 42 minutes

2 teaspoons olive oil

1 large green bell pepper, chopped

2 medium ribs of celery, leaves discarded, sliced

1 medium onion, chopped

1 medium fresh jalapeño, seeds and ribs discarded, chopped

3 medium garlic cloves, minced

1 tablespoon chili powder

1½ teaspoons ground cumin

¼ teaspoon pepper (coarsely ground preferred)

1 15.5-ounce can no-salt-added dark red kidney beans, rinsed and drained

1 15.5-ounce can no-salt-added pinto beans, rinsed and drained

1 15.5-ounce can no-salt-added black beans, rinsed and drained

1 14.5-ounce can no-salt-added diced tomatoes, undrained

1 cup water

2 medium green onions, sliced

1. Heat the oil in the pressure cooker on sauté. Cook the bell pepper, celery, onion, and jalapeño for 5 minutes, or until the bell pepper and celery are tender and the onion is very soft, stirring frequently. Add the garlic. Cook for 30 seconds, stirring frequently. Turn off the pressure cooker.

2. Add the chili powder, cumin, and pepper. Stir well. Stir in the remaining ingredients except the green onions. Secure the lid. Cook on high pressure for 7 minutes. Allow the pressure to release naturally for 10 minutes, then quickly release any remaining pressure. Ladle the chili into bowls. Sprinkle with the green onions.

SERVES 6; 1 cup per serving

PER SERVING Calories 242 / Total Fat 2.0 g Saturated Fat 0.5 g Trans Fat 0.0 g Polyunsaturated Fat 0.5 g Monounsaturated Fat 1.0 g / Cholesterol 0 mg / Sodium 49 mg / Carbohydrates 44 g / Fiber 11 g / Sugars 11 g / Protein 14 g / Dietary Exchanges 2½ starch, 1 vegetable, 1½ lean meat

BROCCOLI-CAULIFLOWER MAC 'N' CHEESE

Broccoli and cauliflower offer a healthy dose of veggies in this two-cheese, ooey-gooey family favorite. It's so easy and delicious, you'll never go back to the boxed kind again.

Total prep, cooking, and pressure release time: 22 minutes

3 cups water

2 cups broccoli florets, cut into bite-size pieces

2 cups cauliflower florets, cut into bite-size pieces

8 ounces whole-grain elbow macaroni

½ teaspoon salt

1 cup shredded low-fat Cheddar cheese

¾ cup fat-free milk

1 ounce low-fat American cheese, cut into pieces

1. In the pressure cooker, stir together the water, broccoli, cauliflower, pasta, and salt. Secure the lid. Cook on high pressure for 4 minutes. Quickly release the pressure. Remove the pressure cooker lid.

2. Set the pressure cooker to sauté. Add the Cheddar, milk, and American cheese, stirring until the cheeses are melted. Turn off the pressure cooker. Remove the pressure cooker lid. Let stand for 5 minutes.

COOK'S TIP: If you prefer a thicker macaroni and cheese, let it stand for 10 to 15 minutes at the end of the cooking time.

SERVES 6; 1 generous cup per serving

PER SERVING Calories 202 / Total Fat 3.0 g Saturated Fat 1.0 g Trans Fat 0.0 g Polyunsaturated Fat 0.5 g Monounsaturated Fat 1.0 g / Cholesterol 6 mg / Sodium 411 mg / Carbohydrates 33 g / Fiber 6 g / Sugars 4 g / Protein 13 g / Dietary Exchanges 2 starch, 1 vegetable, 1 lean meat

SUN-DRIED TOMATO, SPINACH, and QUINOA SALAD

Classic Mediterranean ingredients elevate the flavor of this ancient grain.

Total prep, cooking, and pressure release time: 22 minutes

½ cup dry-packed sun-dried tomatoes, chopped

1 cup boiling water and 2 cups water, divided use

1 teaspoon olive oil and 1 tablespoon olive oil, divided use

1½ cups uncooked quinoa, rinsed and drained

2 tablespoons fresh lemon juice

1 medium garlic clove, minced

⅛ teaspoon crushed red pepper flakes

12 ounces spinach or arugula (about 3 cups loosely packed), coarsely chopped

2 tablespoons unsalted pine nuts or sliced almonds, dry-roasted

1. Put the sun-dried tomatoes in a small bowl. Pour 1 cup boiling water over them. Set aside.

2. Heat 1 teaspoon oil in the pressure cooker on sauté. Cook the quinoa until lightly toasted, stirring constantly. Pour in the remaining 2 cups water. Stir. Secure the lid. Cook on high pressure for 1 minute. Allow the pressure to release naturally.

3. Transfer the quinoa to a large bowl. Drain the sun-dried tomatoes well. Pat dry with paper towels. Stir into the quinoa.

4. In a small bowl, whisk together the lemon juice, garlic, red pepper flakes, and the remaining 1 tablespoon oil.

5. Stir the spinach into the quinoa mixture. Drizzle the dressing over all. Sprinkle with the pine nuts. Serve at room temperature for peak flavor.

SERVES 4; 1½ cups per serving

PER SERVING Calories 338 / **Total Fat** 11.0 g **Saturated Fat** 1.5 g **Trans Fat** 0.0 g **Polyunsaturated Fat** 3.5 g **Monounsaturated Fat** 5.0 g / **Cholesterol** 0 mg / **Sodium** 76 mg / **Carbohydrates** 49 g / **Fiber** 7 g / **Sugars** 5 g / **Protein** 13 g / **Dietary Exchanges** 3 starch, 1 vegetable, 2 fat

LENTIL SLOPPY JOES

Even without the ground beef, this sloppy Joe still has all the flavor and uses lentils to give the dish the heartiness of meat. While this is a great open-face sandwich, it's equally tasty served in a bowl minus the bun.

Total prep, cooking, and pressure release time: 53 minutes

2 cups dried green lentils, sorted for stones and shriveled lentils, rinsed, and drained

1 14.5-ounce can no-salt-added diced tomatoes, undrained

2 medium carrots, finely chopped

1 cup water

½ cup finely chopped onion

3 tablespoons firmly packed brown sugar

2 tablespoons cider vinegar

½ teaspoon chili powder

½ teaspoon paprika

½ teaspoon ground cumin

½ teaspoon dry mustard

¼ teaspoon salt

2 whole-grain hamburger buns (lowest sodium available), split and toasted

1. In the pressure cooker, stir together all the ingredients except the buns. Secure the lid. Cook on high pressure for 20 minutes. Allow the pressure to release naturally for 10 minutes, then quickly release any remaining pressure.

2. Put the bun halves on plates. Spoon the lentil mixture onto the buns.

SERVES 4; 1½ cups lentil mixture and ½ bun per serving

PER SERVING Calories 500 / Total Fat 1.5 g Saturated Fat 0.0 g Trans Fat 0.0 g Polyunsaturated Fat 0.5 g Monounsaturated Fat 0.5 g / Cholesterol 0 mg / Sodium 306 mg / Carbohydrates 96 g / Fiber 17 g / Sugars 24 g / Protein 32 g / Dietary Exchanges 5½ starch, 2 vegetable, 3 lean meat

CHICKPEA TABBOULEH SALAD

This cool summery salad is perfect to pack for a picnic or serve at a barbecue since there's no mayo in it and you don't need to worry about it sitting out for a while.

Total prep, cooking, and pressure release time: 1 hour 25 minutes

5 cups water

1½ cups dried chickpeas, sorted for stones and shriveled peas, rinsed, and drained

2 large tomatoes, seeded and chopped

⅔ cup minced fresh Italian (flat-leaf) parsley

½ large red onion, chopped

½ cup minced fresh mint

8 kalamata olives, rinsed, dried, pitted, and chopped

2 tablespoons fresh lemon juice

1 tablespoon olive oil

1. Combine the water and chickpeas in the pressure cooker. Secure the lid. Cook on high pressure for 45 minutes. Release the pressure naturally for 15 minutes, then quickly release the remaining pressure.

2. Drain the chickpeas in a colander. Rinse the chickpeas under cold running water. Drain well. Transfer the chickpeas to a large bowl. Stir in the remaining ingredients, tossing gently. Serve the salad at room temperature.

SERVES 4; 1½ cups per serving

PER SERVING Calories 343 / Total Fat 9.5 g Saturated Fat 1.0 g Trans Fat 0.0 g Polyunsaturated Fat 2.5 g Monounsaturated Fat 5.0 g / Cholesterol 0 mg / Sodium 154 mg / Carbohydrates 51 g / Fiber 14 g / Sugars 12 g / Protein 16 g / Dietary Exchanges 1 vegetable, 3 starch, 1 lean meat, 1½ fat

LOUISIANA RED BEANS and RICE

This vegetarian version of traditional Louisiana fare is equally delicious without the added fat and sodium from andouille sausage that's usually included. Enjoy with a dark green, leafy salad for a complete meal.

Total prep, cooking, and pressure release time: 1 hour 58 minutes

2 teaspoons canola or corn oil

2 medium ribs of celery, leaves discarded, sliced

1 medium onion, chopped

1 medium green bell pepper, diced

4 cups water

1 pound dried red beans, sorted for stones and shriveled beans, rinsed, and drained

1 14.5-ounce can no-salt-added diced tomatoes, undrained

2 tablespoons salt-free Cajun or Creole seasoning blend

3 medium garlic cloves, minced

½ cup uncooked brown rice

1. Heat the oil in the pressure cooker on sauté. Cook the celery, onion, and bell pepper for 3 minutes, or until the onion is soft, stirring frequently. Turn off the pressure cooker. Stir in the water, beans, tomatoes with liquid, seasoning blend, and garlic. Secure the lid. Cook on high pressure for 50 minutes. Allow the pressure to release naturally for 10 minutes, then quickly release any remaining pressure.

2. Meanwhile, prepare the rice using the package directions, omitting the salt and margarine.

3. Spoon the rice into serving bowls. Spoon the beans and cooking liquid over the rice.

SERVES 6; 1 cup red bean mixture and ¼ cup rice per serving

PER SERVING Calories 363 / Total Fat 2.0 g Saturated Fat 0.0 g Trans Fat 0.0 g Polyunsaturated Fat 0.5 g Monounsaturated Fat 1.0 g / Cholesterol 0 mg / Sodium 49 mg / Carbohydrates 64 g / Fiber 21 g / Sugars 9 g / Protein 21 g / Dietary Exchanges 4 starch, 1 vegetable, 1½ lean meat

BEAN CASSOULET

A cassoulet is a traditional French dish of beans and a variety of meats that's seasoned with herbs. This vegetarian version captures the rich flavor, but thanks to the pressure cooker, is ready to serve (even using dried beans) in about an hour.

Total prep, cooking, and pressure release time: 1 hour 44 minutes

4 cups water

1 cup dried Great Northern beans, sorted for stones and shriveled beans, rinsed, and drained

1½ cups fat-free, low-sodium vegetable broth, such as on page 41

2 medium potatoes, peeled and cut into 1-inch cubes

1 medium onion, cut into 8 wedges

1 medium fennel bulb, quartered and cored

1 tablespoon red wine vinegar

4 medium garlic cloves, minced

1 teaspoon dried oregano, crumbled

¼ teaspoon pepper (coarsely ground preferred)

⅛ teaspoon crushed red pepper flakes

8 ounces spinach (about 2 cups loosely packed), coarsely chopped

1. In the pressure cooker, stir together the water and beans. Secure the lid. Cook on high pressure for 25 minutes. Allow the pressure to release naturally. Turn off the pressure cooker.

2. Drain the beans in a colander. Return to the pressure cooker. Stir in the remaining ingredients except the spinach. Secure the lid. Cook on high pressure for 6 minutes. Allow the pressure to release naturally. Remove the pressure cooker lid.

3. Set the pressure cooker to sauté. Heat the cassoulet until simmering. Stir in the spinach. Cook for 3 minutes, or until the spinach is tender, stirring occasionally.

COOK'S TIP ON FENNEL: Its large base or bulb can be served as a vegetable, while the flowing fronds are excellent when snipped and used as an herb. To prepare the fennel bulb, cut the fronds and trim the stalks from the bulb. Cut the bulb into quarters, stem to root end, then trim out the core. Both the bulb and fronds are delicious served raw or cooked.

SERVES 4; 1½ cups per serving

PER SERVING Calories 241 / Total Fat 1.0 g Saturated Fat 0.0 g Trans Fat 0.0 g Polyunsaturated Fat 0.5 g
Monounsaturated Fat 0.0 g / Cholesterol 0 mg / Sodium 88 mg / Carbohydrates 48 g / Fiber 13 g /
Sugars 3 g / Protein 14 g / Dietary Exchanges 2½ starch, 2 vegetable, 1 lean meat

MUSHROOM-PARMESAN RISOTTO

Risotto can be made with ease in a pressure cooker. This dish is done in minutes and there's no standing over the stove constantly stirring.

Total prep, cooking, and pressure release time: 27 minutes

2 teaspoons olive oil

1 small onion, chopped

8 ounces brown (cremini) mushrooms, cut into thick slices

1 cup uncooked Arborio rice

2 medium garlic cloves, minced

2 cups fat-free, low-sodium vegetable broth, such as on page 41

½ cup dry white wine (regular or nonalcoholic) or water

¾ cup shredded or grated Parmesan cheese

2 tablespoons minced fresh Italian (flat-leaf) parsley

1. Heat the oil in the pressure cooker on sauté. Cook the onion for 3 minutes, or until soft, stirring frequently. Add the mushrooms. Cook for 5 to 7 minutes, or until the mushrooms have released all their liquid, stirring frequently. Stir in the rice and garlic. Cook for 3 minutes, stirring frequently.

2. Pour the broth and wine into the cooker. Using a spoon, stir until all the rice is submerged in the liquid. Secure the lid. Cook on high pressure for 6 minutes. Quickly release the pressure. Stir in the Parmesan. Just before serving, sprinkle with the parsley.

COOK'S TIP: This risotto also makes the perfect side dish to serve 8 and accompany roast chicken, beef, or pork.

SERVES 4; 1¼ cups per serving

PER SERVING Calories 293 / Total Fat 7.0 g Saturated Fat 3.0 g Trans Fat 0.0 g Polyunsaturated Fat 0.5 g
Monounsaturated Fat 3.0 g / Cholesterol 11 mg / Sodium 272 mg / Carbohydrates 44 g / Fiber 3 g /
Sugars 3 g / Protein 13 g / Dietary Exchanges 2½ starch, 1 vegetable, 1 lean meat, ½ fat

AUTUMN FARRO and BUTTERNUT SQUASH

Farro, an ancient grain, is tasty in salads, casseroles, and pilafs. When the nutty, chewy kernels are combined with the sweet goodness of butternut squash, the combination is irresistible.

Total prep, cooking, and pressure release time: 29 minutes

2 teaspoons olive oil

1 small onion, chopped

1 cup uncooked semi-pearled farro

2 cups fat-free, low-sodium vegetable broth, such as on page 41

1 medium butternut squash, peeled and cut into 2-inch cubes

½ teaspoon dried thyme, crumbled

¼ teaspoon salt

¼ teaspoon pepper (coarsely ground preferred)

¼ cup unsalted chopped walnuts, dry-roasted

¼ cup crumbled low-fat feta cheese

1. Heat the oil in the pressure cooker on sauté. Cook the onion for 3 minutes, or until soft, stirring frequently. Add the farro. Cook for 2 to 3 minutes, or until the farro is lightly toasted, stirring frequently. Turn off the pressure cooker.

2. Stir in the broth. Place the steaming rack over the farro. Place the squash on the rack. Sprinkle with the thyme, salt, and pepper. Secure the lid. Cook on high pressure for 8 minutes. Quickly release the pressure.

3. Spoon the squash into a serving bowl. Add the farro, stirring gently to combine. Sprinkle with the walnuts and feta.

COOK'S TIP ON FARRO: Pearled or semi-pearled means that the tough, outer husk of the kernel has been removed or at least partially scratched to make cooking go a little faster.

SERVES 4; 1½ cups per serving

PER SERVING Calories 323 / Total Fat 8.0 g Saturated Fat 1.5 g Trans Fat 0.0 g Polyunsaturated Fat 4.0 g Monounsaturated Fat 2.5 g / Cholesterol 3 mg / Sodium 335 mg / Carbohydrates 50 g / Fiber 6 g / Sugars 4 g / Protein 12 g / Dietary Exchanges 3½ starch, ½ lean meat, 1 fat

MUJADDARA

Mujaddara, a dish of lentils and brown rice, is a popular Middle Eastern comfort food. This dish is so easy to prepare and relies on pantry ingredients, so it's sure to be an entrée you'll prepare again and again.

Total prep, cooking, and pressure release time: 58 minutes

1 tablespoon canola or corn oil

1 medium onion, chopped

1½ cups uncooked brown rice

2 medium garlic cloves, minced

3 cups water

¾ cup dried lentils, sorted for stones and shriveled lentils, rinsed, and drained

¾ teaspoon ground cumin

¼ teaspoon salt

¼ teaspoon pepper (coarsely ground preferred)

1. Heat the oil in the pressure cooker on sauté. Cook the onion for 3 minutes, or until soft, stirring frequently. Stir in the rice. Cook for 5 minutes, or until the rice is toasted and the onion has begun to caramelize, stirring frequently. Stir in the garlic. Cook for 30 seconds, stirring frequently. Turn off the pressure cooker.

2. Stir in the remaining ingredients. Secure the lid. Cook on high pressure for 15 minutes. Allow the pressure to release naturally.

SERVES 6; 1 cup per serving

PER SERVING Calories 291 / Total Fat 4.0 g Saturated Fat 0.5 g Trans Fat 0.0 g Polyunsaturated Fat 1.0 g Monounsaturated Fat 2.0 g / Cholesterol 0 mg / Sodium 110 mg / Carbohydrates 54 g / Fiber 7 g / Sugars 4 g / Protein 12 g / Dietary Exchanges 3½ starch, 1 lean meat

PINTO BEANS
with Cumin and Spinach

The earthiness of the beans complements the savory flavors of ground cumin and spinach.

Total prep, cooking, and pressure release time: 1 hour 3 minutes

4⅓ cups water

2⅔ cups dried pinto beans, sorted for stones and shriveled beans, rinsed, and drained

2¼ teaspoons ground cumin

2 teaspoons chili powder

2 medium garlic cloves, minced

12 ounces spinach (about 3 cups loosely packed), chopped

¼ teaspoon salt

1. In the pressure cooker, stir together the water and beans. Stir in the cumin, chili powder, and garlic. Secure the lid. Cook on high pressure for 30 minutes. Allow the pressure to release naturally. Remove the pressure cooker lid.

2. Set the pressure cooker to sauté. Heat until simmering. Stir in the spinach and salt. Cook for 3 minutes, or until the spinach is wilted, stirring occasionally.

SERVES 6; 1 cup per serving

PER SERVING Calories 309 / Total Fat 2.0 g Saturated Fat 0.5 g Trans Fat 0.0 g Polyunsaturated Fat 0.5 g Monounsaturated Fat 0.5 g / Cholesterol 0 mg / Sodium 165 mg / Carbohydrates 56 g / Fiber 20 g / Sugars 1 g / Protein 20 g / Dietary Exchanges 3½ starch, 2 lean meat

CURRIED CAULIFLOWER
with Chickpeas

The vegetables and legumes in this dish are bathed in a curry-flavored broth.
Serve with Easy Mango Chutney (page 160).

Total prep, cooking, and pressure release time: 1 hour 34 minutes

3 cups water

¾ cup dried chickpeas, sorted for stones and shriveled peas, rinsed, and drained

2 teaspoons canola or corn oil

1 medium onion, chopped

1 medium red bell pepper, chopped

2 tablespoons minced peeled gingerroot

3 medium garlic cloves, minced

1½ cups fat-free, low-sodium vegetable broth, such as on page 41

1 medium head of cauliflower, cut into bite-size florets

2 tablespoons curry powder

¼ teaspoon salt

2 tablespoons minced fresh cilantro (optional)

1. In the pressure cooker, stir together the water and chickpeas. Secure the lid. Cook on high pressure for 45 minutes. Release the pressure naturally for 15 minutes, then quickly release the remaining pressure. Drain the chickpeas in a colander.

2. Heat the oil in the pressure cooker on sauté. Cook the onion for 3 minutes, or until soft, stirring frequently. Add the bell pepper. Cook for 3 minutes, or until tender. Stir in the gingerroot and garlic. Cook for 30 seconds, stirring frequently. Turn off the pressure cooker.

3. Stir in the broth, cauliflower, curry powder, and salt. Stir in the chickpeas. Secure the lid. Cook on high pressure for 3 minutes. Quickly release the pressure.

4. Serve sprinkled with the cilantro.

COOK'S TIP: Curry powder is an integral part of this dish and the actual flavor and heat level vary with the brand. If the brand you're using is labeled "Madras," it's hotter than regular curry powder. Once you make this dish, you'll know if you prefer to increase or decrease the amount of curry powder.

SERVES 4; 1½ cups per serving

PER SERVING Calories 224 / Total Fat 5.5 g Saturated Fat 0.5 g Trans Fat 0.0 g Polyunsaturated Fat 1.5 g Monounsaturated Fat 2.0 g / Cholesterol 0 mg / Sodium 211 mg / Carbohydrates 37 g / Fiber 11 g / Sugars 10 g / Protein 11 g / Dietary Exchanges 1½ starch, 3 vegetable, ½ lean meat

CUBAN-STYLE BLACK BEANS

This is a protein-packed meal that's complete when served with a crisp, dark green salad.

Total prep, cooking, and pressure release time: 1 hour 40 minutes

2 teaspoons canola or corn oil

1 medium onion, chopped

7 cups water

2½ cups dried black beans, sorted for stones and shriveled beans, rinsed, and drained

1 tablespoon ground cumin

2 medium dried bay leaves

4 medium garlic cloves, minced

1 teaspoon dried oregano, crumbled

¼ teaspoon crushed red pepper flakes

1. Heat the oil in the pressure cooker on sauté. Cook the onion for 3 minutes, or until soft, stirring frequently. Turn off the pressure cooker.

2. Stir in the remaining ingredients. Secure the lid. Cook on high pressure for 55 minutes. Release the pressure naturally. Discard the bay leaves before serving.

SERVES 6; 1 cup per serving

PER SERVING Calories 283 / Total Fat 3.0 g Saturated Fat 0.5 g Trans Fat 0.0 g Polyunsaturated Fat 1.0 g Monounsaturated Fat 1.0 g / Cholesterol 0 mg / Sodium 13 mg / Carbohydrates 49 g / Fiber 18 g / Sugars 2 g / Protein 18 g / Dietary Exchanges 3 starch, 2 lean meat

ITALIAN WHEAT BERRY CASSEROLE

Traditional Italian flavors season the whole grain and meatless crumbles in this recipe. Serve with Roman-Style Artichokes (page 153) to complete this meal.

Total prep, cooking, and pressure release time: 1 hour 5 minutes

3 cups water and ⅓ cup water, divided use

1 cup uncooked wheat berries

2 teaspoons olive oil

1 medium onion, chopped

½ medium red or green bell pepper, chopped

2 medium garlic cloves, minced

2 cups frozen meatless crumbles

1 14.5-ounce can diced no-salt-added tomatoes, undrained

2 tablespoons minced fresh Italian (flat-leaf) parsley

1½ teaspoons dried Italian seasoning, crumbled

¼ cup shredded or grated Parmesan cheese

1. In the pressure cooker, stir together 3 cups water and the wheat berries. Secure the lid. Cook on high pressure for 25 minutes. Quickly release the pressure. Turn off the pressure cooker. Drain the wheat berries in a colander.

2. Heat the oil in the pressure cooker on sauté. Cook the onion for 3 minutes, or until soft, stirring frequently. Add the bell pepper and wheat berries. Cook for 5 minutes, or until the wheat berries are toasted, stirring frequently. Add the garlic. Cook for 30 seconds, stirring frequently. Turn off the pressure cooker.

3. Stir in the meatless crumbles, tomatoes with liquid, parsley, Italian seasoning, and the remaining ⅓ cup water. Secure the lid. Cook on high pressure for 4 minutes. Quickly release the pressure.

4. Sprinkle the wheat berry mixture with the Parmesan. Let stand, covered, for 3 minutes, or until the Parmesan has melted.

COOK'S TIP ON WHEAT BERRIES: Wheat berries are the whole, unprocessed kernels of wheat. This whole grain can be quickly cooked in the pressure cooker on high pressure for 25 to 30 minutes. Once cooked, you can serve them as a cereal, a pilaf, or a salad.

SERVES 4; 1½ cups per serving

PER SERVING Calories 318 / Total Fat 5.0 g Saturated Fat 1.5 g Trans Fat 0.0 g Polyunsaturated Fat 0.5 g Monounsaturated Fat 2.0 g / Cholesterol 4 mg / Sodium 312 mg / Carbohydrates 54 g / Fiber 12 g / Sugars 7 g / Protein 23 g / Dietary Exchanges 3 starch, 2 vegetable, 2 lean meat

Vegetables & Side Dishes

MAPLE-GLAZED SWEET POTATOES
with Crunchy Pecan-Oat Streusel

Sweet potatoes with a sweet and nutty crunch make a great autumnal side dish for Spiced Brisket with Cranberries (page 106) or German Pork and Cabbage (page 114).

Total prep, cooking, and pressure release time: 26 minutes

1 cup water

½ teaspoon ground cinnamon and ½ teaspoon ground cinnamon, divided use

2 medium sweet potatoes, peeled and cut into ½-inch slices

2 medium sweet apples, such as Red Delicious, peeled and each cut into 8 wedges

½ cup unsalted chopped pecans, dry-roasted

¼ cup all-purpose flour

3 tablespoons uncooked old-fashioned rolled oats

2 tablespoons firmly packed dark brown sugar

2 tablespoons pure maple syrup

1/16 teaspoon salt

1. In the pressure cooker, stir together the water and ½ teaspoon cinnamon. Place the steaming rack in the cooker.

2. Arrange the sweet potato slices on the rack. Place the apples on the sweet potatoes. Secure the lid. Cook on high pressure for 8 minutes. Quickly release the pressure.

3. In a small bowl, stir together the remaining ingredients, including the remaining ½ teaspoon cinnamon, until well blended. Sprinkle over the sweet potatoes and apples. Cook, covered, on sauté for 3 minutes. (Make sure the pressure valve is left open and the unit is set on sauté only.)

4. Using a spatula, carefully transfer the sweet potatoes and toppings to a platter.

SERVES 6; ½ cup per serving

PER SERVING Calories 217 / Total Fat 7.0 g Saturated Fat 0.5 g Trans Fat 0.0 g Polyunsaturated Fat 2.0 g Monounsaturated Fat 4.0 g / Cholesterol 0 mg / Sodium 67 mg / Carbohydrates 38 g / Fiber 4 g / Sugars 18 g / Protein 3 g / Dietary Exchanges 1½ starch, 1 fruit, 1 fat

Maple-Glazed Sweet
Potatoes with Crunchy
Pecan-Oat Streusel, page 139

Pistachio-Cranberry
Brussels Sprouts, page 142

PISTACHIO-CRANBERRY BRUSSELS SPROUTS

The tang from the cranberries and the crunch of the pistachios add pizzazz to this dish. Try them with Turkey with Sage and Sweet Potatoes (page 94).

Total prep, cooking, and pressure release time: 23 minutes

2 teaspoons olive oil

2 small shallots, diced

1 pound 4 ounces brussels sprouts, trimmed and loose outer leaves discarded

½ cup water

⅓ cup unsweetened dried cranberries

¼ cup shredded or grated Parmesan cheese

3 tablespoons unsalted pistachios, coarsely chopped

1. Heat the oil in the pressure cooker on sauté. Cook the shallots for 2 to 3 minutes, or until soft, stirring frequently. Turn off the pressure cooker. Add the brussels sprouts and water. Secure the lid. Cook on high pressure for 3 minutes. Quickly release the pressure. Turn off the pressure cooker.

2. Stir in the cranberries. Let stand, covered, for 2 minutes. Spoon the brussels sprouts mixture into a serving bowl. Sprinkle with the Parmesan and pistachios.

SERVES 8; ½ cup per serving

PER SERVING Calories 76 / Total Fat 3.5 g Saturated Fat 1.0 g Trans Fat 0.0 g Polyunsaturated Fat 0.5 g Monounsaturated Fat 1.5 g / Cholesterol 2 mg / Sodium 61 mg / Carbohydrates 10 g / Fiber 4 g / Sugars 2 g / Protein 4 g / Dietary Exchanges 2 vegetable, ½ fat

BROCCOLINI
with Lemon and Almonds

The flavor of broccolini, a cross between broccoli and Chinese kale, is enhanced in this dish by the tartness of citrus and the crunchiness of nuts. Serve with Herbed Fish with Vegetables (page 61) or Salmon en Papillote (page 64).

Total prep, cooking, and pressure release time: 7 minutes

¾ cup water

8 ounces broccolini

2 to 3 teaspoons grated lemon zest

2 tablespoons fresh lemon juice

¼ cup unsalted sliced almonds, dry-roasted

1. Place the steaming rack in the pressure cooker. Pour in the water.

2. Place the broccolini on the rack. Secure the lid. Cook on steam for 1 minute. Quickly release the pressure. Turn off the pressure cooker.

3. Using a slotted spoon, transfer the broccolini to a plate. Using potholders, remove the steaming rack. Discard the cooking liquid. Return the broccolini to the pressure cooker. Set the cooker to sauté. Add the lemon zest and lemon juice. Cook for 30 seconds to 1 minute, or until heated through, stirring constantly. Just before serving, sprinkle with the almonds.

COOK'S TIP: If you prefer more tender broccolini, cook on steam for 2 minutes.

SERVES 4; ½ cup per serving

PER SERVING Calories 54 / Total Fat 3.0 g Saturated Fat 0.0 g Trans Fat 0.0 g Polyunsaturated Fat 0.5 g Monounsaturated Fat 2.0 g / Cholesterol 0 mg / Sodium 19 mg / Carbohydrates 6 g / Fiber 2 g / Sugars 1 g / Protein 3 g / Dietary Exchanges 1 vegetable, ½ fat

MEXICAN STREET CORN
with Quinoa

This easy and healthy version of a food sold by street vendors skips the mayo and bumps up the nutrition. Serve with Salsa Chicken Tacos (page 90) or Pork Tacos with Pineapple Salsa (page 115).

Total prep, cooking, and pressure release time: 21 minutes

2 teaspoons canola or corn oil

16 ounces frozen whole-kernel corn (no need to thaw)

1 cup uncooked quinoa, rinsed and drained

1 medium fresh jalapeño, seeds and ribs discarded, finely chopped

½ teaspoon chili powder

¼ teaspoon salt

1¼ cups water

½ cup minced fresh cilantro and (optional) 1 tablespoon minced fresh cilantro, divided use

2 medium green onions, chopped

2 tablespoons fresh lime juice

3 tablespoons low-fat Cotija cheese

1. Heat the oil in the pressure cooker on sauté. Cook the corn for 4 to 6 minutes, or until it begins to crisp, stirring frequently. Add the quinoa, jalapeño, chili powder, and salt. Stir in the water. Secure the lid. Cook on high pressure for 3 minutes. Quickly release the pressure.

2. Stir in ½ cup cilantro, the green onions, and lime juice. Spoon into a serving bowl. Sprinkle with the Cotija cheese. Garnish with the remaining 1 tablespoon cilantro.

SERVES 8; ½ cup per serving

PER SERVING Calories 156 / Total Fat 3.5 g Saturated Fat 0.5 g Trans Fat 0.0 g Polyunsaturated Fat 1.5 g Monounsaturated Fat 1.0 g / Cholesterol 2 mg / Sodium 111 mg / Carbohydrates 28 g / Fiber 4 g / Sugars 4 g / Protein 5 g / Dietary Exchanges 2 starch

CREAMY MASHED POTATOES

Potatoes, a good source of potassium, make the perfect side dish for roast chicken or pot roast. Try these with Pork Loin with Fennel and Mustard (page 111).

Total prep, cooking, and pressure release time: 28 minutes

2 pounds Yukon Gold or yellow potatoes, peeled and cut into 1-inch cubes

¼ teaspoon salt

¼ cup fat-free milk

2 tablespoons fat-free sour cream

1. In the pressure cooker, stir together the potatoes and salt. Pour in cold water to cover the potatoes by 1 inch. Secure the lid. Cook on high pressure for 8 minutes. Quickly release the pressure.

2. In a small microwaveable bowl, microwave the milk on 100 percent power (high) for 40 seconds.

3. Drain the potatoes in a colander. Return to the pressure cooker. Stir in the hot milk and sour cream. Using a potato masher, mash all the ingredients together until smooth. Serve immediately.

4. If not serving immediately, set the pressure cooker on keep warm. Let stand, covered. Serve the potatoes within an hour.

SERVES 8; ½ cup per serving

PER SERVING Calories 94 / Total Fat 0.0 g Saturated Fat 0.0 g Trans Fat 0.0 g Polyunsaturated Fat 0.0 g Monounsaturated Fat 0.0 g / Cholesterol 1 mg / Sodium 86 mg / Carbohydrates 21 g / Fiber 3 g / Sugars 2 g / Protein 3 g / Dietary Exchanges 1½ starch

LIMA BEANS
in Red Wine Vinaigrette

Thanks to a sweet-tart vinaigrette, these limas are bathed in flavor. Enjoy with Spiced Brisket with Cranberries (page 106).

Total prep, cooking, and pressure release time: 43 minutes

3 cups water

⅔ cup dried baby lima beans, sorted for stones and shriveled beans, rinsed, and drained

½ medium onion, chopped, and ½ medium onion, chopped, divided use

½ medium rib of celery, leaves discarded, chopped, and ½ medium rib of celery, leaves discarded, chopped, divided use

½ medium carrot, chopped, and ½ medium carrot, chopped, divided use

¼ cup red wine vinegar

1 tablespoon plus 1 teaspoon olive oil (extra virgin preferred)

2 teaspoons honey

2 teaspoons Dijon mustard (lowest sodium available)

¼ teaspoon salt

¼ teaspoon pepper (coarsely ground preferred)

1. In the pressure cooker, stir together the water, beans, ½ onion, chopped, ½ rib of celery, chopped, and ½ carrot, chopped. Secure the lid. Cook on high pressure for 12 minutes. Allow the pressure to release naturally. Remove the pressure cooker lid.

2. Set on sauté. Heat until simmering. Stir the remaining ½ onion, chopped, ½ rib of celery, chopped, and ½ carrot, chopped, into the bean mixture. Cook for 3 minutes, or until the celery and carrot are tender-crisp, stirring frequently.

3. Drain the beans and vegetables well in a colander (discard any liquid). Transfer to a serving bowl.

4. In a small bowl, whisk together the remaining ingredients. Pour the vinaigrette over the bean mixture, tossing gently to coat.

SERVES 4; generous ½ cup vegetables and 1 tablespoon plus 2 teaspoons vinaigrette per serving

PER SERVING Calories 160 / Total Fat 5.0 g Saturated Fat 0.5 g Trans Fat 0.0 g Polyunsaturated Fat 0.5 g Monounsaturated Fat 3.5 g / Cholesterol 0 mg / Sodium 220 mg / Carbohydrates 24 g / Fiber 7 g / Sugars 9 g / Protein 7 g / Dietary Exchanges 1 starch, 1 vegetable, 1 lean meat

BEET SALAD with Citrus Vinaigrette

Pressure cooking beets is quicker than roasting them. Yet the flavor is just as delicious. The honey-mustard drizzle, which has a hint of tartness from orange zest, complements the sweetness of the cooked beets. Try this with Salmon with Bok Choy (page 67).

Total prep, cooking, and pressure release time: 33 minutes

¾ cup water

¼ cup fresh orange juice and ⅓ cup fresh orange juice, divided use

1 tablespoon grated orange zest

4 medium unpeeled beets (about 3 ounces each), stems trimmed to about 1 inch

8 cups torn mixed salad greens

2 medium navel oranges, peeled and divided into segments

1 medium shallot, finely chopped

½ teaspoon Dijon mustard (lowest sodium available)

½ teaspoon honey

¼ teaspoon pepper (coarsely ground preferred)

1 teaspoon olive oil (extra virgin preferred)

¼ cup unsalted chopped pistachios, dry-roasted

¼ cup low-fat goat cheese crumbles

1. Pour the water and ¼ cup orange juice into the pressure cooker. Place the steaming rack in the cooker. Place the beets on the rack. Secure the lid. Cook on high pressure for 18 minutes. Quickly release the pressure.

2. Remove the beets. Let cool. When cool enough to handle, wearing disposable plastic gloves (to keep from staining your fingers), peel off and discard the skins using your fingers or a paring knife. Thinly slice the beets.

3. Arrange the salad greens on plates. Top with the beets and orange segments.

4. In a small bowl, whisk together the remaining ⅓ cup orange juice, the orange zest, shallot, mustard, honey, and pepper. Whisk in the oil until combined.

5. Drizzle the dressing over each salad. Garnish with the pistachios and goat cheese crumbles.

SERVES 4; 2 cups greens, 1 beet, and 2 tablespoons dressing per serving

PER SERVING Calories 175 / Total Fat 6.5 g Saturated Fat 1.5 g Trans Fat 0.0 g Polyunsaturated Fat 1.5 g Monounsaturated Fat 2.5 g / Cholesterol 3 mg / Sodium 171 mg / Carbohydrates 26 g / Fiber 7 g / Sugars 16 g / Protein 7 g / Dietary Exchanges 1 fruit, 2 vegetable, ½ lean meat, 1 fat

DOWN-HOME "BAKED" BEANS

Thick and richly flavored thanks to the molasses, this recipe will remind you of classic oven-baked beans even though they really aren't baked. Enjoy these beans with Chicago Beef Sandwiches (page 102).

Total prep, cooking, and pressure release time: 1 hour 20 minutes

1½ cups water

¾ cup dried navy beans, sorted for stones and shriveled beans, rinsed, and drained

1 cup chopped onion

½ cup chopped green bell pepper

2 tablespoons molasses

1 teaspoon dry mustard

½ teaspoon paprika (smoked preferred)

½ teaspoon pepper (coarsely ground preferred)

¼ teaspoon salt

1. In the pressure cooker, stir together the water and beans. Secure the lid. Cook on high pressure for 22 minutes. Allow the pressure to release naturally.

2. Stir in the remaining ingredients. Secure the lid. Cook on high pressure for 5 minutes. Allow the pressure to release naturally. Remove the pressure cooker lid.

3. Set the pressure cooker to sauté. Heat until simmering. Cook for 2 to 3 minutes, or until the bean mixture thickens to the desired consistency, stirring occasionally.

SERVES 4; ½ cup per serving

PER SERVING Calories 184 / Total Fat 1.0 g Saturated Fat 0.0 g Trans Fat 0.0 g Polyunsaturated Fat 0.0 g Monounsaturated Fat 0.0 g / Cholesterol 0 mg / Sodium 160 mg / Carbohydrates 36 g / Fiber 11 g / Sugars 12 g / Protein 10 g / Dietary Exchanges 1½ starch, 1 vegetable, ½ other carbohydrate, 1 lean meat

HONEY-CUMIN GLAZED ROOT VEGETABLES

A simple seasoning highlighting cumin and honey are all these earthy vegetables need. Serve with Gingered Pork Tenderloin with Plums (page 113).

Total prep, cooking, and pressure release time: 20 minutes

2 medium turnips (about 5 ounces each), peeled and cut into 6 wedges

2 medium parsnips (about 4 ounces each), peeled and cut into 2-inch pieces

1 medium carrot, cut into 1-inch pieces

½ teaspoon ground cumin

¼ teaspoon salt

¼ teaspoon pepper (coarsely ground preferred)

½ cup fat-free, low-sodium vegetable broth, such as on page 41

1 tablespoon honey

1. Put the turnips, parsnips, and carrot in the pressure cooker. In a small bowl, stir together the cumin, salt, and pepper. Sprinkle over the vegetables. Pour the broth around the vegetables. Secure the lid. Cook on high pressure for 2 minutes. Quickly release the pressure.

2. Using a slotted spoon, transfer the vegetables to a serving bowl.

3. Set the pressure cooker to sauté. Stir the honey into the liquid in the pressure cooker. Cook for 2 to 3 minutes, or until the liquid is reduced by half. Drizzle the honey mixture over the vegetables.

COOK'S TIP ON CARROTS AND PARSNIPS: Carrots typically would take longer to cook in a pressure cooker than the parsnips. By cutting the carrots into smaller pieces, the vegetables will cook more uniformly. Also, parsnips have a thicker stem end and taper to a thinner point. If the tip is very thin, cut that end of the parsnip in slightly larger pieces so they too will cook more uniformly.

SERVES 4; ½ cup per serving

PER SERVING Calories 86 / Total Fat 0.5 g Saturated Fat 0.0 g Trans Fat 0.0 g Polyunsaturated Fat 0.0 g Monounsaturated Fat 0.0 g / Cholesterol 0 mg / Sodium 208 mg / Carbohydrates 21 g / Fiber 5 g / Sugars 10 g / Protein 2 g / Dietary Exchanges 1 starch, ½ other carbohydrate

ROMAN-STYLE ARTICHOKES

This Italian-inspired dish pairs perfectly with entrées such as Mushroom-Parmesan Risotto (page 129) or Italian Wheat Berry Casserole (page 137).

Total prep, cooking, and pressure release time: 25 minutes

2 whole artichokes

½ cup dry white wine (regular or nonalcoholic); fat-free, low-sodium chicken broth or Chicken Stock, such as on page 39; or water

½ cup water

2 tablespoons chopped fresh Italian (flat-leaf) parsley

2 medium garlic cloves, minced

½ teaspoon dried oregano, crumbled

¼ teaspoon salt

1 tablespoon olive oil (extra virgin preferred)

1. Working with one artichoke at a time, peel off and discard the tough outer leaves. Trim 1 inch from the top. Discard. Trim off any fibrous parts. Discard. Halve each artichoke lengthwise. Using a spoon, scrape out the fuzzy choke portion. Discard.

2. Pour the wine and water into the pressure cooker. Place the steaming rack in the cooker. Arrange the artichoke halves with the cut side up on the rack.

3. In a small bowl, stir together the parsley, garlic, oregano, and salt. Sprinkle over the artichokes. Secure the lid. Cook on high pressure for 10 minutes. Quickly release the pressure.

4. Transfer the artichokes to a platter. Drizzle with the oil.

SERVES 4; ½ artichoke per serving

PER SERVING Calories 64 / Total Fat 3.5 g Saturated Fat 0.5 g Trans Fat 0.0 g Polyunsaturated Fat 0.5 g Monounsaturated Fat 2.5 g / Cholesterol 0 mg / Sodium 207 mg / Carbohydrates 8 g / Fiber 4 g / Sugars 1 g / Protein 2 g / Dietary Exchanges 1 vegetable, 1 fat

Sauces & More

MARINARA SAUCE

Pressure cooking marinara provides an intense burst of flavor in a short amount of time. Use this healthier version (in place of jarred store-bought spaghetti sauces) over whole-grain pasta or in your favorite Italian dishes.

Total prep, cooking, and pressure release time: 1 hour 15 minutes

2 teaspoons olive oil

1 large onion, chopped

4 medium garlic cloves, minced

1 28-ounce can no-salt-added crushed tomatoes, undrained

½ cup dry red wine (regular or nonalcoholic)

½ cup water

2 medium dried bay leaves

1½ teaspoons dried basil, crumbled

½ teaspoon dried oregano, crumbled

½ teaspoon dried thyme, crumbled

¼ teaspoon crushed red pepper flakes

¼ teaspoon salt

¼ teaspoon pepper (coarsely ground preferred)

1. Heat the oil in the pressure cooker on sauté. Cook the onion for 3 minutes, or until soft, stirring frequently. Add the garlic. Cook for 30 seconds, stirring frequently. Turn off the pressure cooker.

2. Stir in the remaining ingredients until blended. Secure the lid. Cook on high pressure for 25 minutes. Allow the pressure to release naturally for 25 minutes, then quickly release any remaining pressure. Discard the bay leaves before serving.

COOK'S TIP: This recipe freezes well. Pour or spoon the sauce into airtight freezer containers that are labeled with the date. Use the sauce within four to six months.

SERVES 10; ½ cup per serving

PER SERVING Calories 50 / Total Fat 1.0 g Saturated Fat 0.0 g Trans Fat 0.0 g Polyunsaturated Fat 0.0 g Monounsaturated Fat 0.5 g / Cholesterol 0 mg / Sodium 73 mg / Carbohydrates 8 g / Fiber 2 g / Sugars 4 g / Protein 2 g / Dietary Exchanges 2 vegetable

MIDDLE EASTERN EGGPLANT SAUCE

Turmeric and cinnamon, spices common in Middle Eastern dishes, flavor this distinctive eggplant sauce. Serve this sauce over cooked whole-grain couscous. Garnish with crumbled low-fat feta cheese for a delicious dinner.

Total prep, cooking, and pressure release time: 58 minutes

2 teaspoons olive oil

1 medium onion, chopped

4 medium garlic cloves, minced

1 medium eggplant (about 1 pound), peeled and cut into ½- to ¾-inch cubes

1 28-ounce can no-salt-added crushed tomatoes, undrained

1 6-ounce can no-salt-added tomato paste

2 tablespoons minced fresh Italian (flat-leaf) parsley

1 tablespoon red wine vinegar

½ teaspoon ground turmeric

¼ teaspoon ground cinnamon

¼ teaspoon salt

¼ teaspoon pepper (coarsely ground preferred)

1. Heat the oil in the pressure cooker on sauté. Cook the onion for 3 minutes, or until soft, stirring frequently. Add the garlic. Cook for 30 seconds, stirring frequently. Stir in the eggplant. Cook for 3 minutes, stirring frequently. Turn off the pressure cooker.

2. Stir in the remaining ingredients. Secure the lid. Cook on high pressure for 15 minutes. Allow the pressure to release naturally.

COOK'S TIP ON EGGPLANT: There are many varieties of eggplant, but the most common is a dark purple eggplant that's somewhat pear-shaped. Choose one that's firm with a glossy skin. Peeling the eggplant gives it a milder flavor. Once exposed, the flesh discolors quickly, so cut it just before cooking.

SERVES 10; ½ cup per serving

PER SERVING Calories 67 / Total Fat 1.0 g Saturated Fat 0.0 g Trans Fat 0.0 g Polyunsaturated Fat 0.0 g Monounsaturated Fat 0.5 g / Cholesterol 0 mg / Sodium 83 mg / Carbohydrates 13 g / Fiber 4 g / Sugars 7 g / Protein 3 g / Dietary Exchanges 3 vegetable

CINNAMON-SPICE APPLESAUCE

The sweetness of cinnamon, ginger, and nutmeg complements the tartness of the apples to create a comforting flavor and an unforgettable aroma as they cook together. Serve with roasted chicken or pork, German Pork and Cabbage (page 114), or Turkey with Sage and Sweet Potatoes (page 94).

Total prep, cooking, and pressure release time: 44 minutes

8 apples, such as Braeburn, Cortland, Jonathan, McIntosh, or Winesap, peeled and coarsely diced

½ cup 100% apple juice

1 tablespoon fresh lemon juice

1 teaspoon ground cinnamon

½ teaspoon ground ginger

¼ teaspoon ground nutmeg

1. Put all the ingredients in the pressure cooker. Secure the lid. Cook on high pressure for 4 minutes. Allow the pressure to release naturally.

2. Using a potato masher, mash the apple mixture to the desired consistency (coarse or smooth texture).

SERVES 8; ½ cup per serving

PER SERVING Calories 86 / Total Fat 0.5 g Saturated Fat 0.0 g Trans Fat 0.0 g Polyunsaturated Fat 0.0 g Monounsaturated Fat 0.0 g / Cholesterol 0 mg / Sodium 1 mg / Carbohydrates 23 g / Fiber 2 g / Sugars 18 g / Protein 1 g / Dietary Exchanges 1½ fruit

STRAWBERRY-RHUBARB SAUCE

This sauce is perfect to spoon over fat-free, sugar-free vanilla Greek yogurt. It makes an excellent topping for whole-grain waffles, too.

Total prep, cooking, and pressure release time: 34 minutes

8 ounces frozen unsweetened whole strawberries

8 ounces frozen rhubarb slices

⅓ cup 100% white grape juice

¼ cup sugar

1 cinnamon stick (about 3 inches long) or ½ teaspoon ground cinnamon

¼ teaspoon ground ginger

1 tablespoon cornstarch

2 tablespoons cold water

1. Put the strawberries, rhubarb, grape juice, sugar, cinnamon stick, and ginger in the pressure cooker. Secure the lid. Cook on high pressure for 3 minutes. Release the pressure naturally for 15 minutes, then quickly release any remaining pressure. Remove the pressure cooker lid.

2. Discard the cinnamon stick.

3. Set the pressure cooker to sauté. Heat until the liquid is simmering. Put the cornstarch in a small bowl. Add the water, whisking to dissolve. Stir the cornstarch mixture into the sauce until blended. Cook for about 1 minute, or until the sauce thickens, stirring constantly.

COOK'S TIP: Serve the sauce warm or cold. Cover and refrigerate it for up to two weeks.

SERVES 8; ¼ cup per serving

PER SERVING Calories 51 / Total Fat 0.0 g Saturated Fat 0.0 g Trans Fat 0.0 g Polyunsaturated Fat 0.0 g
Monounsaturated Fat 0.0 g / Cholesterol 0 mg / Sodium 2 mg / Carbohydrates 13 g / Fiber 1 g /
Sugars 9 g / Protein 0 g / Dietary Exchanges ½ fruit, ½ other carbohydrate

EASY MANGO CHUTNEY

Chutney, which originated in India, is a spicy condiment made of fruits or vegetables mixed with vinegar, spices, and sugar. Spoon this homemade chutney over roasted or grilled meat or poultry, add it to a sandwich, dollop it on a piece of cheese, or stir it into fat-free plain Greek yogurt.

Total prep, cooking, and pressure release time: 36 minutes

3 medium mangoes, peeled, pitted, and chopped

1 small red onion, finely chopped

1 small red bell pepper, finely chopped

¼ cup golden raisins

¼ cup cider vinegar

3 tablespoons firmly packed dark brown sugar

2 tablespoons minced peeled gingerroot

¼ teaspoon ground cinnamon

¼ teaspoon crushed red pepper flakes

¼ teaspoon salt

¼ teaspoon pepper (coarsely ground preferred)

In the pressure cooker, stir together all the ingredients. Secure the lid. Cook on high pressure for 6 minutes. Allow the pressure to release naturally for 10 minutes, then quickly release any remaining pressure.

COOK'S TIP: Tightly cover and refrigerate the chutney. Use it within two weeks. For longer storage, spoon it into airtight freezer containers and freeze.

COOK'S TIP ON MANGOES: Select ripe mangoes by choosing one that yields to light pressure, but isn't overripe. To cut and peel a mango, first slice off the bottom so it sits vertically. Cut down with a sharp knife, sliding along the hard seed in the middle of the fruit. Repeat on the other side of the seed. Using the tip of the knife, cut the flesh on each piece crosswise and lengthwise, not cutting through the peel. Gently arch the peel backward to reveal cubes of fruit. Cut the cubes away from the peel. Then, cut away the fruit that clings to the seed; peel and chop it.

SERVES 16; 2 tablespoons per serving

PER SERVING Calories 61 / Total Fat 0.5 g Saturated Fat 0.0 g Trans Fat 0.0 g Polyunsaturated Fat 0.0 g Monounsaturated Fat 0.0 g / Cholesterol 0 mg / Sodium 39 mg / Carbohydrates 15 g / Fiber 1 g / Sugars 13 g / Protein 1 g / Dietary Exchanges ½ fruit, ½ other carbohydrate

Breakfast Dishes

WARM FRUIT COMPOTE

Warm fruit compote infused with classic autumnal spices, such as cinnamon and nutmeg, is perfect on its own or on top of a scoop of fat-free, sugar-free vanilla frozen yogurt.

Total prep, cooking, and pressure release time: 24 minutes

10 ounces unsweetened dried fruit

¾ cup water

2 tablespoons firmly packed brown sugar

1 teaspoon honey

½ teaspoon ground cinnamon

Dash of ground nutmeg

3 tablespoons unsalted sliced almonds, dry-roasted

1. In the pressure cooker, stir together the fruit, water, brown sugar, honey, cinnamon, and nutmeg. Secure the lid. Cook on high pressure for 4 minutes. Allow the pressure to release naturally for 10 minutes, then quickly release any remaining pressure.

2. Serve the compote warm. Sprinkle with the almonds.

SERVES 4; ½ cup fruit and 2 tablespoons liquid per serving

PER SERVING Calories 247 / Total Fat 2.5 g Saturated Fat 0.0 g Trans Fat 0.0 g Polyunsaturated Fat 0.5 g Monounsaturated Fat 1.5 g / Cholesterol 0 mg / Sodium 6 mg / Carbohydrates 54 g / Fiber 4 g / Sugars 38 g / Protein 4 g / Dietary Exchanges 3½ fruit, ½ fat

YOGURT PARFAITS

If you have a yogurt setting on your multicooker, you'll want to experience making homemade yogurt; just be sure to allow plenty of time before you want to serve these parfaits. It's not that it's difficult, it just takes several hours in the multicooker to make.

Total prep, cooking, and pressure release time: 33 minutes

4 cups Homemade Fat-Free Yogurt (recipe on page 165)

1 tablespoon honey

½ teaspoon vanilla extract

1⅓ cups raspberries, blackberries, or sliced hulled strawberries

¼ cup unsalted chopped pistachios, dry-roasted

1. Place the yogurt in a fine-mesh sieve set over a bowl. Transfer to the refrigerator. Allow to drain for 30 minutes, to thicken slightly.

2. In a small bowl, whisk together the yogurt, honey, and vanilla.

3. In each parfait glass, spoon equal amounts of the yogurt and raspberries, alternating the layers. Garnish with the pistachios.

SERVES 4; 1 cup yogurt and ⅓ cup fruit per serving

PER SERVING Calories 167 / Total Fat 4.0 g Saturated Fat 0.5 g Trans Fat 0.0 g Polyunsaturated Fat 1.0 g Monounsaturated Fat 2.0 g / Cholesterol 5 mg / Sodium 106 mg / Carbohydrates 24 g / Fiber 3 g / Sugars 19 g / Protein 11 g / Dietary Exchanges 1 fat-free milk, ½ fruit, 1 fat

MAKES 7 CUPS OF FAT-FREE YOGURT

PER SERVING Calories 97 / Total Fat 0.0 g Saturated Fat 0.0 g Trans Fat 0.0 g Polyunsaturated Fat 0.0 g Monounsaturated Fat 0.0 g / Cholesterol 6 mg / Sodium 120 mg / Carbohydrates 14 g / Fiber 0 g / Sugars 14 g / Protein 10 g / Dietary Exchanges 1 low-fat milk

Homemade Fat-Free Yogurt

Making your own yogurt is easy, and you'll enjoy the fresh flavor, too. Not only can you take pride in making it yourself, but you won't find surprising ingredients hidden in the ingredient list. Enjoy it as is or sweeten it by adding the fruits you enjoy most.

Total prep, cooking, and pressure release time: 8 hours 36 minutes

2 quarts fat-free milk (pasteurized, but not Ultra High Temperature [UHT] pasteurized)

2 tablespoons plain yogurt (with live cultures)

1. Pour the milk into the pressure cooker. Cover, with the vent closed, and set to the yogurt setting. Adjust the temperature to indicate boil. Heat the milk for 20 to 30 minutes, or until the temperature registers 180°F on an instant-read thermometer, whisking frequently.

2. Meanwhile, fill a sink with ice water.

3. When the milk registers the proper temperature, immediately remove the lid. Transfer the cooking pot to the icy water. Let the milk cool for 5 minutes, or until the temperature registers between 110°F and 115°F on an instant-read thermometer, whisking frequently.

4. In a small bowl, whisk together ½ cup warm milk and the yogurt, until smooth and well blended. Stir the milk mixture into the warm milk in the cooking pot. Return the cooking pot to the pressure cooker. Secure the lid and close the vent. Cook on the yogurt setting for 8 hours.

5. Spoon the yogurt into a bowl. Cover and refrigerate for 8 hours, or up to one week. (The yogurt will thicken a bit as it chills.) Use for Yogurt Parfaits (page 164) and any of your favorite recipes that call for plain yogurt.

COOK'S TIPS ON MAKING YOGURT: Draining the yogurt thickens it. If you want a thicker yogurt that's similar to commercially prepared Greek yogurt, drain the yogurt (in a fine-mesh sieve over a bowl in the refrigerator) for up to 8 hours.

Fat-free milk typically makes a thinner yogurt than whole milk. If you'd like it to be thicker, stir 1 cup fat-free dry milk powder into the milk when you first begin to heat it.

When making homemade yogurt, monitor the temperature of the milk and use an accurate instant-read thermometer. The times are only estimates.

See opposite page for nutritional information.

MAPLE-PUMPKIN SPICE STEEL-CUT OATS

Maple syrup and pumpkin go together and make early-morning wake-up calls easier. Steel-cut oats have the perfect texture and are a satisfying way to begin the day.

Total prep, cooking, and pressure release time: 37 minutes

4 cups water

1½ cups uncooked steel-cut oats

¾ cup canned solid-pack pumpkin (not pie filling)

2 tablespoons firmly packed dark brown sugar

2 tablespoons pure maple syrup

1½ teaspoons pumpkin pie spice

¼ teaspoon salt

1 cup fat-free milk

3 tablespoons unsalted chopped pecans, dry-roasted

1. In the pressure cooker, stir together the water, oats, pumpkin, brown sugar, maple syrup, pumpkin pie spice, and salt. Secure the lid. Set on the porridge setting. Cook on high pressure for 12 minutes. Allow the pressure to release naturally for 10 minutes, then quickly release any remaining pressure.

2. Remove the pressure cooker lid. Stir in the milk. Serve the oatmeal warm. Sprinkle with the pecans.

COOK'S TIP: If you don't have pumpkin pie spice, you can use a blend of 1 teaspoon ground cinnamon, ¼ teaspoon ground ginger, ⅛ teaspoon ground cloves, and ⅛ teaspoon ground nutmeg.

COOK'S TIP ON DRY-ROASTING NUTS: Dry-roasting nuts intensifies their flavor. Spread them in a single layer on a baking sheet. Bake at 350°F for 5 to 7 minutes, or until lightly toasted. Or, put the nuts in a single layer in a small skillet. Dry-roast them over medium heat for about 4 minutes, or until just fragrant, stirring frequently.

SERVES 6; 1 cup per serving

PER SERVING Calories 244 / Total Fat 5.5 g Saturated Fat 0.5 g Trans Fat 0.0 g Polyunsaturated Fat 1.5 g Monounsaturated Fat 2.5 g / Cholesterol 1 mg / Sodium 122 mg / Carbohydrates 41 g / Fiber 10 g / Sugars 12 g / Protein 8 g / Dietary Exchanges 2 starch, 1 other carbohydrate, 1 fat

SOUTHERN-STYLE GRITS

Cheesy, creamy grits are a traditional Southern favorite. If you've never tasted grits, this recipe will make you a fan. Enjoy as an accompaniment to eggs for a protein-rich start to your morning.

Total prep, cooking, and pressure release time: 36 minutes

2 teaspoons canola or corn oil

1 cup stone-ground grits

3 cups water

1¼ cups fat-free milk

1 cup shredded low-fat Cheddar cheese

¼ teaspoon salt

Heat the oil in the pressure cooker on sauté. Cook the grits for 5 minutes, or until toasted, stirring frequently. Stir in the remaining ingredients. Secure the lid. Cook on high pressure for 10 minutes. Allow the pressure to release naturally for 10 minutes, then quickly release any remaining pressure.

SERVES 8; ½ cup per serving

PER SERVING Calories 126 / Total Fat 2.5 g Saturated Fat 1.0 g Trans Fat 0.0 g Polyunsaturated Fat 0.5 g Monounsaturated Fat 1.0 g / Cholesterol 4 mg / Sodium 179 mg / Carbohydrates 19 g / Fiber 1 g / Sugars 2 g / Protein 6 g / Dietary Exchanges 1½ starch

BLUEBERRY JEWELED OATMEAL

Is there anything as warm, nourishing, and comforting as oatmeal in the morning? Top it with pops of fresh blueberries and this breakfast favorite will be at the top of your "must have often" list.

Total prep, cooking, and pressure release time: 35 minutes

4½ cups water

1½ cups uncooked steel-cut oats

¼ cup firmly packed dark brown sugar

½ teaspoon ground cinnamon

¼ teaspoon salt

1½ cups blueberries

1 cup fat-free milk

1. In the pressure cooker, stir together the water, oats, brown sugar, cinnamon, and salt. Secure the lid. Set on the porridge setting. Cook on high pressure for 12 minutes. Allow the pressure to release naturally for 10 minutes, then quickly release any remaining pressure.

2. Remove the pressure cooker lid. Stir in the blueberries and milk. Serve warm.

SERVES 6; 1 cup per serving

PER SERVING Calories 231 / Total Fat 3.0 g Saturated Fat 0.0 g Trans Fat 0.0 g Polyunsaturated Fat 1.0 g Monounsaturated Fat 1.0 g / Cholesterol 1 mg / Sodium 122 mg / Carbohydrates 44 g / Fiber 9 g / Sugars 15 g / Protein 8 g / **Dietary Exchanges** 2 starch, ½ fruit, ½ other carbohydrate

POTATO-HERB HASH with Eggs

Once a common dish, hash was typically made with leftover cooked potatoes, meat, and vegetables. With a pressure cooker, you no longer need to wait for leftovers; you can enjoy this hearty breakfast dish in just minutes.

Total prep, cooking, and pressure release time: 18 minutes

2 teaspoons canola or corn oil

½ medium onion, chopped

4 medium russet potatoes, peeled or unpeeled, and cut into ½-inch cubes

½ medium red or green bell pepper, chopped

⅔ cup fat-free, low-sodium vegetable broth (such as on page 41)

2 tablespoons minced fresh Italian (flat-leaf) parsley and 2 teaspoons minced fresh Italian (flat-leaf) parsley, divided use

½ teaspoon dried tarragon, crumbled

½ teaspoon pepper (coarsely ground preferred)

⅛ teaspoon salt

4 large eggs

1. Heat the oil in the pressure cooker on sauté. Cook the onion for 3 minutes, or until soft, stirring frequently. Turn off the pressure cooker.

2. Stir in the potatoes, bell pepper, broth, 2 tablespoons parsley, the tarragon, pepper, and salt. Secure the lid. Cook on high pressure for 3 minutes. Quickly release the pressure. Turn off the pressure cooker.

3. Remove the lid of the pressure cooker. Crack one egg into a small bowl. Using the back of a spoon, make a small well in the potatoes, pushing the potatoes aside. Slip the egg into the well. Repeat with the remaining 3 eggs, making a separate well for each. Secure the lid with the pressure vent open. Cook on sauté for 2 minutes. If the eggs aren't cooked to the desired consistency, re-cover the pressure cooker. Let stand on keep warm for 2 to 3 minutes, or until the eggs are cooked to the desired consistency. Serve the hash sprinkled with the remaining 2 teaspoons parsley.

COOK'S TIP: You can substitute 2 small to medium sweet potatoes for 2 of the russet potatoes in this dish. The combination of potatoes is both beautiful and tasty. Omit the tarragon or replace it with dried thyme.

SERVES 4; 1 cup per serving

PER SERVING Calories 237 / Total Fat 7.5 g Saturated Fat 2.0 g Trans Fat 0.0 g Polyunsaturated Fat 1.5 g Monounsaturated Fat 3.5 g / Cholesterol 186 mg / Sodium 161 mg / Carbohydrates 33 g / Fiber 5 g / Sugars 3 g / Protein 10 g / Dietary Exchanges 2 starch, 1 lean meat, ½ fat

DENVER OMELET

One taste of this omelet and it'll be your new weekend go-to breakfast dish. Add a fresh fruit and whole-wheat toast for a satisfying and nutritious meal to start your day off right.

Total prep, cooking, and pressure release time: 31 minutes

Cooking spray

1 teaspoon canola or corn oil

⅓ cup chopped onion

⅓ cup chopped green bell pepper

⅓ cup chopped red bell pepper

3 ounces diced low-sodium, low-fat ham, all visible fat discarded

2 cups water

4 large eggs

2 large egg whites

½ cup low-fat shredded Cheddar cheese

1. Lightly spray a 4-cup heatproof glass dish with cooking spray.

2. Heat the oil in the pressure cooker on sauté. Cook the onion, bell peppers, and ham for 3 minutes, or until the onion is soft, stirring frequently. Transfer the mixture to a bowl. Turn off the pressure cooker.

3. Place the steaming rack in the pressure cooker. Pour in the water.

4. In a bowl, whisk together the eggs and egg whites until well blended. Stir in the Cheddar and cooked onion mixture. Pour into the glass dish.

5. Place the dish with the egg mixture on the steaming rack. Secure the lid. Cook on high pressure for 8 minutes. Quickly release the pressure.

6. Using potholders, carefully remove the dish from the cooker. Let stand for 10 minutes before serving.

COOK'S TIP: You can use 1 cup of vegetables that you may have on hand in place of the onion and bell peppers.

SERVES 4; 1 wedge (one quarter of the omelet) per serving

PER SERVING Calories 150 / Total Fat 7.5 g Saturated Fat 2.5 g Trans Fat 0.0 g Polyunsaturated Fat 1.5 g Monounsaturated Fat 3.0 g / Cholesterol 198 mg / Sodium 363 mg / Carbohydrates 4 g / Fiber 1 g / Sugars 2 g / Protein 15 g / Dietary Exchanges 2 lean meat

Denver Omelet,
page 171

BROCCOLI FRITTATA

A frittata is an Italian omelet in which eggs and other ingredients are cooked together. It's a versatile dish and while often served for breakfast, a frittata can also be served for lunch or as a simple supper dish. Serve with fresh fruit and whole-wheat toast for a complete breakfast.

Total prep, cooking, and pressure release time: 37 minutes

2 cups water

Cooking spray

2 large eggs

4 large egg whites

1½ cups finely chopped broccoli

1 shallot, finely minced

½ teaspoon dried basil, crumbled

¼ teaspoon pepper (coarsely ground preferred)

3 tablespoons shredded or grated Parmesan cheese and 2 tablespoons shredded or grated Parmesan cheese, divided use

1. Place the steaming rack in the pressure cooker. Pour in the water. Lightly spray a 7-cup round glass baking dish with cooking spray.

2. In a medium bowl, whisk together the eggs and egg whites until combined. Stir in the broccoli, shallot, basil, and pepper. Stir in 3 tablespoons Parmesan. Pour the broccoli mixture into the baking dish. Cover the dish with aluminum foil.

3. Place the dish with the broccoli mixture in the center of a foil sling. To make a foil sling, cut an 18-inch-long piece of aluminum foil. Fold it lengthwise in thirds to make a ribbon about 4 x 18 inches. Draw the ends of the foil up and over the dish. Using the sling, lower the dish onto the rack in the pressure cooker. Secure the lid. Cook on high pressure for 20 minutes. Quickly release the pressure.

4. Using potholders, carefully lift the foil sling supporting the dish out of the pressure cooker. Remove the pressure cooker lid. Sprinkle the frittata with the remaining 2 tablespoons Parmesan. Let stand, covered, for 2 to 3 minutes, or until the Parmesan has melted. Uncover the dish. Cut the frittata into 4 wedges.

SERVES 4; 1 wedge (one quarter of the frittata) per serving

PER SERVING Calories 94 / Total Fat 4.5 g Saturated Fat 2.0 g Trans Fat 0.0 g Polyunsaturated Fat 0.5 g Monounsaturated Fat 1.5 g / Cholesterol 98 mg / Sodium 208 mg / Carbohydrates 4 g / Fiber 1 g / Sugars 1 g / Protein 10 g / Dietary Exchanges 1 vegetable, 1½ meat

BREAKFAST BULGUR, PEAR, and WALNUT PORRIDGE

Ready for a change from oatmeal? Try this hot, hearty cereal made with bulgur, which is wheat kernels that are steamed, dried, and crushed. The nutty flavor of the bulgur contrasts with the sweetness of the pears and is accented with toasted walnuts and cinnamon. Top it off with a dollop of yogurt and breakfast is ready in no time.

Total prep, cooking, and pressure release time: 25 minutes

2⅔ cups water

1⅓ cups uncooked bulgur

1 medium pear, peeled and chopped, and 1 medium pear, peeled and chopped, divided use

½ teaspoon ground cinnamon and ¼ teaspoon ground cinnamon for garnish, divided use

⅓ cup unsalted chopped walnuts, dry-roasted

1 5.3-ounce container fat-free vanilla Greek yogurt

1. In the pressure cooker, stir together the water, bulgur, 1 chopped pear, and ½ teaspoon cinnamon. Secure the lid. Cook on high pressure for 5 minutes. Allow the pressure to release naturally.

2. Spoon the porridge into serving bowls. Top each serving with the remaining 1 chopped pear, the walnuts, and a dollop of yogurt. Sprinkle with the remaining ¼ teaspoon cinnamon.

SERVES 4; 1 cup per serving

PER SERVING Calories 304 / Total Fat 7.0 g Saturated Fat 0.5 g Trans Fat 0.0 g Polyunsaturated Fat 5.0 g Monounsaturated Fat 1.0 g / Cholesterol 0 mg / Sodium 30 mg / Carbohydrates 54 g / Fiber 12 g / Sugars 12 g / Protein 11 g / Dietary Exchanges 2½ starch, 1 fruit, ½ lean meat, 1 fat

RAISIN FRENCH TOAST BAKE

Take a break from the ordinary weekend breakfast fare of pancakes or waffles with this extraordinary version of sweet and nutty French toast. Delicious served warm, you can top it with sliced fresh fruit or berries and a dollop of fat-free yogurt.

Total prep, cooking, and pressure release time: 28 minutes

1½ cups water

Cooking spray

3 large egg whites

1 large egg

½ cup fat-free milk

2 tablespoons sugar

½ teaspoon ground cinnamon

4 slices of whole-wheat raisin bread (lowest sodium available), toasted and cut into ¾-inch squares

3 tablespoons unsalted sliced almonds, dry-roasted

1. Place the steaming rack in the pressure cooker. Pour in the water. Lightly spray a 7-cup heatproof glass bowl with cooking spray.

2. In a bowl, whisk together the egg whites and egg until well blended. Whisk in the milk, sugar, and cinnamon. Gently stir in the bread to coat the squares.

3. Spoon the bread mixture into the glass bowl. Sprinkle the almonds over the bread mixture. Cover the top of the dish with aluminum foil.

4. Place the bowl with the bread mixture in the center of a foil sling. To make a foil sling, cut an 18-inch-long piece of aluminum foil. Fold it lengthwise in thirds to make a ribbon about 4 x 18 inches. Draw the ends of the foil up and over the dish. Using the sling, lower the bowl onto the rack in the pressure cooker. Secure the lid. Cook on high pressure for 16 minutes. Quickly release the pressure.

5. Using potholders, carefully lift the sling supporting the bowl out of the pressure cooker. Uncover the bowl. Cut the bake into wedges. Serve warm.

SERVES 4; 1 wedge (one quarter of the casserole) per serving

PER SERVING Calories 162 / Total Fat 4.5 g Saturated Fat 1.0 g Trans Fat 0.0 g Polyunsaturated Fat 1.0 g Monounsaturated Fat 2.5 g / Cholesterol 47 mg / Sodium 162 mg / Carbohydrates 23 g / Fiber 3 g / Sugars 10 g / Protein 8 g / Dietary Exchanges 1 starch, ½ other carbohydrate, 1 lean meat

Desserts

ALMOND RICE PUDDING
with Fresh Berries

This dessert has it all—creaminess, nuttiness, and tartness. The colorful berries contrast beautifully against the paleness of the pudding.

Total prep, cooking, and pressure release time: 58 minutes

3 cups fat-free milk

¼ cup sugar

½ cup uncooked Arborio rice

1/16 teaspoon salt

2 large eggs, beaten well

¼ teaspoon almond extract or ½ teaspoon vanilla extract

1½ cups raspberries, blueberries, blackberries, or any combination

1. Set the pressure cooker to sauté. Cook the milk and sugar for 2 to 3 minutes, or until the sugar is dissolved, stirring constantly. Stir in the rice and salt. Secure the lid. Cook on high pressure for 10 minutes. Unplug the pressure cooker so that it doesn't switch to keep warm. Allow the pressure to release naturally for 20 minutes, then quickly release any remaining pressure. Remove the pressure cooker lid.

2. In a medium bowl, whisk together the eggs and almond extract. Whisk about 1 cup of the hot rice mixture into the egg mixture. Slowly pour the combined mixture into the pudding. Set the pressure cooker to sauté. Cook the pudding for 3 minutes, or until thickened, stirring constantly.

3. Remove the cooking pot from the pressure cooker. Immediately spoon the pudding into bowls. Place plastic wrap on the surface of each pudding. Refrigerate for at least 15 minutes. Just before serving, top each pudding with ¼ cup raspberries.

SERVES 6; ½ cup pudding and ¼ cup raspberries per serving

PER SERVING Calories 168 / Total Fat 2.0 g Saturated Fat 0.5 g Trans Fat 0.0 g Polyunsaturated Fat 0.5 g Monounsaturated Fat 0.5 g / Cholesterol 65 mg / Sodium 99 mg / Carbohydrates 30 g / Fiber 2 g / Sugars 16 g / Protein 8 g / Dietary Exchanges 1 starch, ½ fat-free milk, ½ other carbohydrate

CHOCOLATE FUDGE CAKE

Warm and gooey chocolate desserts may be all-time favorites. What's the secret to this fudgy treat not only being delicious but healthy? Ingredients like applesauce and egg whites and flavor boosts from unsweetened cocoa make the winning combination in this dessert. Also, the simplicity of using a pressure cooker allows this dessert to be on your table quickly and easily. Enjoy with a cold glass of fat-free milk!

Total prep, cooking, and pressure release time: 47 minutes

1½ cups water and 2 teaspoons boiling water, divided use

Cooking spray

⅔ cup all-purpose flour

⅓ cup unsweetened cocoa powder, 1 teaspoon unsweetened cocoa powder, and (optional) 1 to 2 tablespoons unsweetened cocoa powder for sprinkling, divided use

3 tablespoons plus 2 teaspoons sugar

1 teaspoon baking powder

¼ teaspoon baking soda

½ cup fat-free milk

¼ cup unsweetened applesauce

2 large egg whites

2 tablespoons canola or corn oil

½ teaspoon vanilla extract

1 teaspoon firmly packed dark brown sugar

1. Place the steaming rack in the pressure cooker. Pour in the water.

2. Line a 7-inch springform pan with a sheet of cooking parchment about 12 x 16 inches, folding the parchment to fit snugly across the bottom of the pan and up the side, leaving the edges of the paper above the pan. Lightly spray the parchment with cooking spray.

3. In a small bowl, whisk together the flour, ⅓ cup cocoa, the sugar, baking powder, and baking soda.

4. In a large bowl, whisk together the milk, applesauce, egg whites, oil, and vanilla. Add the flour mixture, stirring until the batter is just moistened but no flour is visible. Pour the batter into the pan.

5. In a small bowl, stir together the remaining 2 teaspoons boiling water, the 1 teaspoon cocoa, and brown sugar until smooth. Drizzle the cocoa mixture over the batter in the pan. Don't stir.

(CONTINUED)

6. Cover the pan with aluminum foil. Place the pan in the center of a foil sling. To make a foil sling, cut an 18-inch-long piece of aluminum foil. Fold it lengthwise in thirds to make a ribbon about 4 x 18 inches. Draw the ends of the foil up and over the pan. Using the sling, lower the pan onto the rack in the pressure cooker. Secure the lid. Cook on high pressure for 22 minutes. Quickly release the pressure.

7. Using potholders, carefully lift the sling supporting the pan out of the pressure cooker. Transfer the pan to a cooling rack. Let cool for 5 minutes. Uncover and remove the sides of the springform pan. The cake will be baked, but softly set.

8. Using a sifter, dust the cake with the remaining 1 to 2 tablespoons cocoa powder. Cut the cake into 6 wedges. Serve warm.

COOK'S TIP: When served warm, the cake will be softly set and fudgy in the center.

SERVES 6; 1 wedge (one sixth of the cake) per serving

PER SERVING Calories 163 / Total Fat 5.5 g Saturated Fat 0.5 g Trans Fat 0.0 g Polyunsaturated Fat 1.5 g Monounsaturated Fat 3.0 g / Cholesterol 0 mg / Sodium 149 mg / Carbohydrates 24 g / Fiber 2 g / Sugars 11 g / Protein 4 g / Dietary Exchanges 1½ other carbohydrate, 1 fat

GINGERBREAD

Molasses, cinnamon, and ginger are the key ingredients in gingerbread. The familiarity of that spicy-sweet blend satisfies and comforts like no other dessert.

Total prep, cooking, and pressure release time: 1 hour 10 minutes

2 cups water and ½ cup hot water, divided use

Cooking spray

¼ cup canola or corn oil

3 tablespoons sugar

¼ cup plus 1 tablespoon molasses

¼ cup egg substitute

1¼ cups all-purpose flour

1 teaspoon ground cinnamon

1 teaspoon ground ginger

¾ teaspoon baking soda

¼ teaspoon salt

1 cup unsweetened applesauce

1. Place a steaming rack in the pressure cooker. Pour in 2 cups water. Line a 7-inch springform pan with a sheet of cooking parchment about 12 x 16 inches, folding the parchment to fit snugly across the bottom of the pan and up the sides, leaving the edges of the paper above the pan. Lightly spray the parchment with cooking spray.

2. In a medium bowl, using an electric mixer on medium speed, beat together the oil and sugar. Add the molasses and egg substitute. Beat until smooth. In a small bowl, whisk together the remaining ingredients except the applesauce. Pour the flour mixture into the molasses mixture. Beat until smooth and no flour is visible. Pour in the remaining ½ cup hot water, beating until well blended. Pour the batter into the pan, gently smoothing the top. Cover the pan with aluminum foil.

3. To make a sling, cut an 18-inch-long piece of aluminum foil. Fold it lengthwise in thirds to make a ribbon about 4 x 18 inches. Place the pan in the center of the sling and draw the ends of the foil up and over the pan. Using the sling, lower the pan onto the rack in the pressure cooker. Secure the lid. Cook on high pressure for 40 minutes. Quickly release the pressure. Using potholders, carefully lift the sling supporting the pan out of the pressure cooker. Transfer the pan to a cooling rack. Let cool for 10 minutes. Uncover and remove the sides of the springform pan. Using a spatula, transfer the gingerbread to a serving plate. Cut into wedges. Dollop with applesauce.

SERVES 12; 1 wedge and 1 tablespoon plus 1 teaspoon applesauce per serving

PER SERVING Calories 137 / Total Fat 5.0 g Saturated Fat 0.5 g Trans Fat 0.0 g Polyunsaturated Fat 1.5 g
Monounsaturated Fat 3.0 g / Cholesterol 0 mg / Sodium 142 mg / Carbohydrates 22 g / Fiber 1 g /
Sugars 11 g / Protein 2 g / Dietary Exchanges 1½ other carbohydrate, 1 fat

PEACH CRISP

Why wait until summer for fresh peaches when you can use the frozen variety instead during any season. Use the slow cooker setting on your electric pressure cooker to make this sunny, ever-popular dessert. You can "set it and forget it" while you're tending to dinner.

Total prep, cooking, and pressure release time: 3 hours 23 minutes

1 pound 8 ounces frozen unsweetened peach slices, slightly thawed

¼ cup firmly packed dark brown sugar

2 tablespoons quick-cooking tapioca

½ teaspoon ground cinnamon

½ cup uncooked quick-cooking oats

⅓ cup unsalted coarsely chopped pecans

2 tablespoons all-purpose flour

2 teaspoons canola or corn oil

1. In a medium bowl, stir together the peaches, brown sugar, tapioca, and cinnamon. Transfer the peach mixture to the pressure cooker. Secure the lid. Set on the slow cooker setting. Cook for 3 hours.

2. Preheat the oven to 375°F.

3. In a small bowl, stir together the oats, pecans, flour, and oil. Spread on a baking sheet. Bake for 10 minutes. Stir. Bake for 8 minutes, or until browned and toasted. Remove from the oven. Set aside until serving time.

4. Ladle the peach mixture into serving dishes. Sprinkle with the oat topping. Serve warm.

SERVES 6; ½ cup peaches and 2½ tablespoons oat topping per serving

PER SERVING Calories 189 / Total Fat 7.0 g Saturated Fat 0.5 g Trans Fat 0.0 g Polyunsaturated Fat 2.5 g Monounsaturated Fat 4.0 g / Cholesterol 0 mg / Sodium 3 mg / Carbohydrates 30 g / Fiber 4 g / Sugars 14 g / Protein 3 g / Dietary Exchanges 2 other carbohydrate, 1½ fat

BAKED APPLES

Apples baking with cinnamon always create an enticing aroma in the kitchen. This dessert is ready at nearly the spur of the moment and tastes just as good as the aroma suggests. These apples are easy to bake while you're eating dinner, and they also make an easy after-school snack for the kids.

Total prep, cooking, and pressure release time: 13 minutes

1 cup 100% apple juice

4 medium unpeeled firm, crisp apples, such as Braeburn, Cameo, Honeycrisp, or Granny Smith (Jonathan or Gala not recommended)

2 tablespoons firmly packed brown sugar

1½ teaspoons ground cinnamon

1. Place a steaming rack in the pressure cooker. Pour in the apple juice.

2. Core the apples from the stem end, but don't cut all the way through the bottom of them. In a small bowl, stir together the brown sugar and cinnamon. Spoon the brown sugar mixture into the center of the apples.

3. Place the apples upright on the steaming rack. Secure the lid. Cook on high pressure for 3 minutes. Quickly release the pressure.

4. Using tongs or a slotted spoon, transfer the apples to dessert bowls. Drizzle each apple with 1 tablespoon hot apple juice. Serve warm.

SERVES 4; 1 apple per serving

PER SERVING Calories 152 / Total Fat 0.5 g Saturated Fat 0.0 g Trans Fat 0.0 g Polyunsaturated Fat 0.0 g Monounsaturated Fat 0.0 g / Cholesterol 0 mg / Sodium 6 mg / Carbohydrates 40 g / Fiber 5 g / Sugars 32 g / Protein 1 g / Dietary Exchanges 2 fruit, ½ other carbohydrate

CRANBERRY POACHED PEARS

When dessert is as beautiful as it is delicious, you know you have a winning recipe. The pears take on a delicate rose hue when poached in cranberry juice flavored with just a touch of ginger and orange.

Total prep, cooking, and pressure release time: 18 minutes

4 firm, but ripe, Bosc pears

1 tablespoon fresh lemon juice

6 cups 100% cranberry juice

2 tablespoons minced peeled gingerroot

2 tablespoons grated orange zest

2 tablespoons sugar

1. Peel the pears, leaving the stems intact. Immediately place the pears in a resealable plastic bag. Drizzle with the lemon juice. Seal the bag. Massage the pears to coat with the juice.

2. In the pressure cooker, stir together the cranberry-cherry juice drink, gingerroot, orange zest, and sugar until well blended. Place the pears in the juice mixture. (Be sure the pears are covered by the juice; if needed, pour in additional juice to cover the pears.)

3. Secure the lid. Cook on high pressure for 3 minutes. Quickly release the pressure.

4. Transfer the pears from the poaching liquid to dessert dishes. Drizzle each serving with 1 tablespoon poaching liquid if desired. Serve warm.

COOK'S TIP ON PEARS: You can use any type of pear for this dessert, but Bosc pears are best as they hold their shape while cooking, making for a more attractive presentation. Bosc pears are easily identified by their elongated necks and a warm golden-russet, almost cinnamon, color.

SERVES 4; 1 pear per serving

PER SERVING Calories 135 / Total Fat 0.5 g Saturated Fat 0.0 g Trans Fat 0.0 g Polyunsaturated Fat 0.0 g Monounsaturated Fat 0.0 g / Cholesterol 0 mg / Sodium 4 mg / Carbohydrates 36 g / Fiber 6 g / Sugars 26 g / Protein 1 g / Dietary Exchanges 2½ fruit

Index

Note that page references in *italics* indicate photographs.

Other cookbooks from the American Heart Association

American
Heart
Association®

Find us online at heart.org

Available everywhere books are sold